The Michigan Historical Reprint Series

Reprints from the collection of the University of Michigan University Library

This volume is produced from digital images created through the University of Michigan University Library's preservation reformatting program. The Library seeks to preserve the intellectual content of items in a manner that facilitates and promotes a variety of uses. The digital reformatting process results in an electronic version of the text that can both be accessed online and used to create new print copies. This book and thousands of others can be found in the digital collections of the University of Michigan Library. The University Library also understands and values the utility of print, and makes reprints available through its Scholarly Publishing Office.

For access to the University of Michigan Library's digital collections, please see http://www.lib.umich.edu.

The Scholarly Publishing Office seeks to disseminate high-quality, cost-effective scholarly content through both print and electronic publishing. Information about the Scholarly Publishing Office can be found at http://spo.umdl.umich.edu.

The Scholarly Publishing Office
the University of Michigan
University Library

GOLD-FOIL,

HAMMERED FROM POPULAR PROVERBS

BY

TIMOTHY TITCOMB,

AUTHOR OF "LETTERS TO THE YOUNG."

"Proverbs are the daughters of daily experience."
Dutch Proverb.

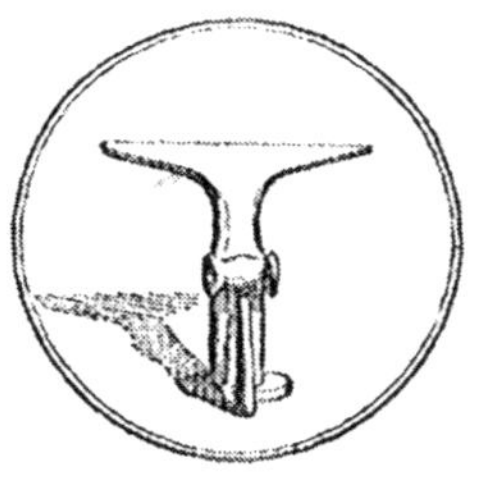

SEVENTEENTH EDITION.

NEW YORK:
CHARLES SCRIBNER, 124 GRAND STREET
1863.

JOHN F. TROW,
Printer, Stereotyper, and Electrotyper,
46, 48 & 50 Greene Street,
Between Grand & Broome, New York.

PREFACE.

THE grass that grows upon the lawn elects and drinks from the juices of the earth the elements that compose its structure; but if the lawn be cropped year after year, and have no return of the materials removed, it will cease to thrive. A wise husbandry will spread upon its surface the results of the life that has been taken away, and these will furnish its most healthful nourishment. So the vital truths, relating to the common life of man, are elected and drawn from soils containing innumerable ingredients that may not be assimilated. Many of these ingredients, good and bad, are furnished by the schools and by the professional mind, and it may legitimately be the work of a layman to take the results of the life that has been lived—the truths that have been verified and vitalized by human experience—and give them again to the soil that has produced them. With the records of popular experience in my hand, as they are embodied in popular proverbs, I aim to do this work in this book.

THE AUTHOR.

SPRINGFIELD, MASS., 1859.

CONTENTS.

GOLD-FOIL.

I.

AN EXORDIAL ESSAY.

"Cold broth hot again, that loved I never;
Old love renewed again, that loved I ever."

"Get thy spindle and thy distaff ready, and God will send thee flax."

FOR the general public, I have written a preface, that the aims and character of my book may be comprehended at a glance, as it is lifted from the shelf of the bookseller; but to those who read the book, I have something more that I wish to say by way of introduction.

It is not for the brilliant brace of initial sermons that we still admire the man whom we love to call "our minister." The old love must be renewed again, from Sabbath to Sabbath, from month to month, and from year to year, by new exhibitions of his power and new demonstrations of his faculty to feed the mo

1*

tives of a large and luxuriant life within our souls. If he fail in this—if his power flinch through laziness, or flag through languor—and he resort to the too common process of heating again the old broth, his productions will grow insipid, and our hungering natures will turn uneasily to other sources for refreshment. It is not for the fresh cheek, the full lip, the fair forehead, the parted sweeps of sunny hair, and the girlish charm of form and features, that we love the wives who have walked hand in hand with us for years, but for new graces, opening each morning like flowers in the parterre, their predecessors having accomplished their beautiful mission and gone to seed. Old love renewed again, through new motives to love, is certainly a thing lovely in itself, and desirable by all whose ambition and happiness it is to sit supreme in a single heart, or to hold an honorable place in the affections of the people.

A few months ago, the pen that traces these lines commenced a series of letters to the young. The letters accumulated, and grew into a book; and this book, with honest aims and modest pretensions, has a place to-day in many thousand homes, while it has been read by hundreds of thousands of men and women in every part of the country. More and better than this, it has become an inspiring, moving and directing power in a great aggregate of young life. I say this with that kind of gladness and gratitude which admits of little pride. I say it because it has been said to me—revealed to me in letters brimming with thankfulness and overflowing with friendliness; expressed to me in silent pressures of the hand—pressures so full of meaning that I involuntarily looked at my palm to see if a jewel had not been left in it; uttered to me by eyes full of interest and pleasure; told to me in plain and homely words in the presence of tears that came unbidden, like so many angels sliding silently out of heaven, to vouch for their honesty. To say that all this makes me happy, would not be to say all that I feel. I account the honor of occupying a pure place in the popular heart—of being welcomed in God's name into the affectionate confidence of those for whom life has high meanings and high issues—of being recognized as among the beneficent forces of society—the greatest honor to be worked for and won under the stars. So much for that which is past, and that which is.

And now, I would have the old love renewed. I would come to the hearts to which the letters have given me access with another gift—with food for appetites quickened and natures craving further inspiration. I would bring new thoughts to be incorporated into individual and social life, which shall strengthen their vital processes, and add to their growth. I would continue and perpetuate the communion of my own with the popular heart. To do this successfully, I know that I must draw directly upon the world's experience, and upon the results of my own individual thinking, acting, living. I know that no truth can be uttered by a soul that has not realized it in some way with hope to be heard. Preceptive wisdom that has not been vivified by life has in itself no affinity for life.

It is a blessed thing that the heart has an instinct which tells it without fail who has the right to teach it. The stricken mother, sitting by the side of the lifeless form of her first-born, will hear unmoved the words of consolation and the persuasions to resignation which are urged by one who has not suffered, even though he eloquently draw motives from the highest heaven; while the silent pressure of her hand by some humble creature who has hidden her treasure under the daisies, will inspire her with calmness and strength. The world cares little for theorists and theories,—little for schools and schoolmen,—little for any thing a man has to utter that has not previously been distilled in the alembic of his life. It is the life in literature that acts upon life. The pilgrim who knocks at the door of the human heart with gloved hands and attire borrowed for the occasion, will meet with tardy welcome and sorry entertainment; but he who comes with shoes worn and dusty with the walk upon life's highway—with face bronzed by fierce suns and muscles knit by conflict with the evils of the passage, will find abundant entrance and hospitable service.

The machinery which I propose to adopt for my purpose is simple enough. It is the habit of the mind to condense into diminutive, agreeable and striking forms the results of experience and observation in all the departments of life. As the carbon, disengaged by fire in its multitudinous offices, crystallizes into a diamond that flashes fire from every facet, and bears at every angle the solvent power of the mother flame; so great clouds of truth are evolved by human experience, which are crystallized at last into proverbs, that flash with the lights of history, and illuminate the darkness which rests upon the track of the future. The proverbs of a nation furnish the index to its spirit and the results of its civilization. As this spirit was kind or unkind—as this civilization was Christian or unchristian—are the proverbs valuable or worthless to us. I know of no more unworthy sentiments, no more dangerous heresies, and no more mischievous lies than are to be found among the proverbs that have received currency, and a permanent record in the world; but here and there among the ignoble paste shine noble gems, and these, as they may seem worthy, I propose to use as textual titles for these new essays of mine. I choose them because they are the offspring of experience—because they are instinct with blood and breath and vitality. They have no likeness to the unverified deductions of reason. They are not propositions, conceived in the understanding and addressed to life, but propositions born of life itself, and addressed to the heart. They were not conceived in the minds of the great few, but they sprang from the life of the people. I give the people their own.

Precisely what these essays of mine are to be, I cannot tell, because I do not know. I only know that there is an inexhaustible realm of practical truth around me waiting for revelation. There are multitudinous thoughts, now trailing upon the ground, that point their tendrils tipped with instinct toward this pen of mine, striving to reach and twine themselves around it that they may be lifted into the sunlight of popular recognition. I have got my spindle and my distaff ready—my pen and mind—never doubting for an instant that God will send me flax. Toward the soul which places itself in the attitude of reception, all things flow. For such a soul are all good gifts fashioned in heaven. The sun shines for it; the birds sing for it; up toward it the flowers swing their censers and waft their odors. Into it in golden streams flows the beauty of star-sprinkled rivers. The roar of waters and the plash of waterfalls give healthful pulse to its atmosphere. Into its open windows come the notes of human joy and human woe in the triumphs and the struggles of the passing time. Past its open door Memory leads the long procession of its precious dead, who look in with sweet faces and whispers of peace. In front of it, Imagination marshals the forces of the future, and it thrills with the bugle-blast and trembles with the drum-beat of the thundering host. For perception were all things made, and to the door of perception all things tend; so that the soul that throws itself wide open to all that is made for it shall find itself full.

When a soul thus receptive places itself in the attitude of expression, it has but to move its lips and the words will flow. The mind that has become a treasure house of truth and beauty speaks a world into existence with every utterance. Expression is its instinct and its necessity. This expression may not always seek the shape of language, but it will assert itself in some form. The patriot reveals the secret of his soul when he gladly dies for his country, and sacrifices his life upon the altar of his inspiration. The Sister of Mercy tells the story of her love and her devotion, unseen and unheard of the world, in midnight ministrations to the comfort of the sick and the dying. The modest mother expresses the love and life she has received from God and the things of God in the tutelage of the young spirits born of her, and the creation of a bright and graceful home for them. We give what we have received—that which is within us wil out of us. Expression is the necessity of possession.

The form which expression takes depends upon natural tendencies and aptitudes, and habits imposed by circumstances and opportunities. I suppose that to every man who writes a book, or is in the habit of writing books, there comes at the conclusion of each effort a sense of exhaustion. Then, through days, and weeks, and months, he walks contentedly, taking in new food—without method, without design—any thing, every thing—regaling his sensibilities, ministering to his appetite for knowledge, exercising his sympathies, absorbing greedily all the influences evolved by the life around him, till there steals upon him, insensibly, the desire for another instalment of expression in the habitual way. He finds himself organizing the truth he has received into harmonious and striking forms. He is arrested in fits of abstraction into which he has fallen unawares. He will not be content until the pen is in his hand, and his mind has applied itself to the work demanded by its condition.

But about the flax that God sends to such a man: this would all seem to be pulled from the earth, softened by sun and rain, and broken and hackled by natural processes. True: and yet I imagine there are few thinking minds in the world that are not aware of a double process by which expression is arrived at—one entirely involuntary, lying deep down in the consciousness, and operated independently of volition; and another, voluntary, lying upon the surface, and mostly engaged in the invention of forms—dependent for materials upon the process beneath it. This is the reason why millions of men undertake to do what they never can do. The involuntary—the divine process—working profoundly in their natures, throws up materials which they have no power to clothe in language, or present in forms of art which the mind will recognize as appropriate. Such men are misled. They strive to write essays, and fail. They struggle to produce poems, but cannot. They have abundant materials for essays and epics in them, but they are incapable of combining and expressing them. Many men and women spend their lives in unsuccessful efforts to spin the flax God sends them upon a wheel they can never use. The trouble with these people is that they have made a mistake in their spindle. It is with the human mind as with the plant. Deep down under ground there is a process of selection going on, by which salts and juices are drawn by a million roots and rootlets into the stem—drawn from masses of mould and sand and gravel—and sent upward to be acted upon again—flax sent up by God to be spun. Every tree and shrub is a distaff for holding, and every twig a spindle for spinning the material with which God invests it. One twig, by a power of its own, will make an apple, another a peach, another a pear, another will spin through long weeks upon a round, green bud, and then weave into it star-beams and moonbeams and sunbeams, and burst into a rose. The man full of juices and rich with life, who was made simply to bear Roxbury Russets, and yet undertakes to bear roses or magnolia blossoms, will always fail. Blessed is that man who knows his own distaff, and has found his own spindle.

It is with the conviction that this pen which I hold is my particular spindle that I begin upon the flax God sends me, through a process entirely independent of my will, and undertake to spin a series of essays, kind readers, for you. That I may be able to contribute a worthy thread to the warp of your lives, or at least to furnish a portion of their woof—contributing to their substance, if not to their beauty—is my warmest wish and my most earnest prayer.

II.

THE INFALLIBLE BOOK.

"He that leaves Certainty and sticks to Chance,
When fools pipe, he may dance."

"Better ride an ass that carries us than a horse that throws us."

WE live in the future. Even the happiness of the present is made up mostly of that delightful discontent which the hope of better things inspires. We lie all our invalid lives by the side of our Bethesda, watching the uneasy quicksand upon its bottom, in its silvery eruptions, and listening to the murmuring gurgle of the retiring streamlet, yet waiting evermore for the angel to come and stir the waters that we may be blest. The angel comes, and the waters are stirred, but not for us; and, though others grasp the blessing which we may not, we look for the angel still, and in this sweet looking fall happily asleep at last, and waken possibly in the angel's arms;—possibly, where? As the future holds our happiness and hopes, so does it also hold our fears and our apprehensions; and the mind is on a constant outlook for that upon which it can best rely to avoid the evils which it dreads, and secure the good which it desires. It reaches in all directions with its hands, and tries in all directions with its feet, for a solid basis of calculation and expectation, with reference to its future pleasure and pain. As the future is inscrutable, it reads carefully the lessons of experience, studies the nature and tendency of things having relation to its life, erects theories and institutes schemes of good, and bends its energies to the achievement and security of protection, necessary ministry, and all desirable possession. All this it does with reference to the few years of mortal life which remain to it.

But there is a God above the soul, and there is something within it which prophesies of another life. The body is to die; so much is certain. What lies beyond? No one who passes the charmed boundary comes back to tell. The imagination visits the realm of shadows—sent out from some window of the soul over life's restless waters—but wings its way wearily back with no olive leaf in its beak as a token of emerging life beyond the closely-bending horizon. The great sun comes and goes in heaven, yet breathes no secret of the ethereal wildernesses. The crescent moon cleaves her nightly passage across the upper deep, but tosses overboard no message, and displays no signals. The sentinel stars challenge each other as they walk their nightly rounds, but we catch no syllable of the countersign which gives passage to the heavenly camp. Shut in! Shut in! Between this life and the other life there is a great gulf fixed, across which neither eye nor foot can travel. The gentle friend whose eyes we closed in their last sleep long years ago, died with rapture in her wonder-stricken eyes, a smile of ineffable joy upon her lips, and hands folded over a triumphant heart; but her lips were past speech, and intimated nothing of the vision that enthralled her.

So, in the lack of all demonstration, we have but one resort, and that is to faith. Faith must build a bridge for us; faith must weave wings for us; and that faith must find materials for its fabrics brought from the other side of the gulf, and not produced on this. We cannot enter the spirit land to explore, record, and report; so all we get must be revealed to us. We may talk never so loudly of the intimations of the immortality within us, of the light of reason and of conscience, of the godlike human soul; we may speculate with marvellous ingenuity upon the future development and destiny of powers that seem angelic even to ourselves, but it is all conjecture—it is all as unsubstantial as the dreams that haunt our slumbers. Unless God teach us of the things of God, or delegate some occupant of a heavenly seat to tell us of the things of heaven and of the destiny of the great family of intelligences to which we belong, we shall know nothing upon these subjects. Briefly, all knowledge concerning the future condition of men must come from the other world to this, and not through any agency initiated in this. We are thus helplessly, inevitably, left to revelation. We cannot help ourselves. We may flutter and flounder under this conviction as much as we choose, but fluttering and floundering avail nothing. If the fact that we are immortal be not revealed to us by a Being who knows, and cannot lie; if the way to make our immortality a happy one be not pointed out to us by one who has the right to direct, then are we in darkness that may be felt—then are we afloat upon a wide sea, without rudder or compass.

Now, there can be no faith in any revelations concerning the future state, and no faith in the things revealed, without a thorough conviction on the part of the soul exercising it that the source from which these revelations come is infallible. They must also be authoritative, and fully received as such into the convictions, or they are nothing. A revelation from any source, touching whose authority the soul admits a doubt, is absolutely valueless as an inspirer of faith. It is for this reason that all the unsettled mind in Christendom is drifting either towards an infallible

Bible, or an infallible church, or an infallible atheism—infallible because denying every thing—shutting God and the future out of existence. With many the drifting process is done with, and the journey is completed in rest and satisfaction. Many can say, with the Bible upon the heart—"This is God's word. It is my rule of life. I believe in the God and the immortality which it reveals. I trust in it, and am happy." Others, educated to believe in an infallible church, or struggling through frightful years of skepticism, have taken refuge in Rome, and tied up to the element of infallibility which they imagine they find there. Others still are either practically or professedly atheists and infidels, discarding Bible and church, and resting, or trying to rest, in the infallibility of a broad negation.

It is not for me to prove the infallibility of the Bible, in part or in whole. I have not undertaken the task in this article, nor do I propose to undertake it in any future article. Neither do I undertake to show that an infallible church cannot be made out of fallible materials. Still less do I undertake to prove the existence of a God and a future life. I take it for granted that the question of a future life is one of great interest to all minds, and the question of its happiness or misery, of the greatest, to most. I assume that the Bible communicates a correct knowledge of God and human duty and destiny, or that nothing whatever is known of them. I assert that in the degree in which this Bible has been received, as a whole and in particulars, as the infallible rule of faith and duty, have those thus receiving it found rest, peace, fearlessness of the future, and hope of everlasting happiness. I affirm that in tho degree in which men have wandered away from this Bible into skepticism, or taken it into their hands to cheapen the character of its inspiration—to cut, and cull, and criticize—have they made themselves and others unhappy. All that has been done to weaken the foundation of an implicit faith in the Bible, as a whole, has been at the expense of the sense of religious obligation, and at the cost of human happiness.

The mind, in such a matter as this, seeks for something reliable, and will have it. If it cannot find it, it will make it. If it will not accept the Bible as such, it will make an infallible church, or deify and enthrone the human reason. One of the most interesting developments of modern spiritualism is the illustration which it gives us of this fact. Tired with the puerile and contradictory revelations which it gets, or supposes it gets, from the spirit world, it has, in multitudes of instances, sunk into a cold rationalism, or thrown itself, disgusted and discouraged, upon the bosom of the Catholic Church, by a very necessity. Now there is no logical tendency of spiritualism into systems so diverse as these It is the instinctive leap of a soul, misled by its intellect, yet true to its wants, out of a jargon of demoniacal whims into something which has, or assumes to have, infallibility. The rush of atheists and infidels into spiritualism—atheists and infidels practical and theoretical—is the rush of a class of minds that find it hard to believe without demonstration, and seek among these necromantic manifestations for something better than its reason, and more readily evident to it than the revelations of the Bible.

I say that toward an infallible Bible, or an infallible church, or an atheism and infidelity growing out of the deification of the human reason, the mind of all unsettled Christendom is drifting, by a necessity of its nature. It will have something upon which it can rely. It cannot abide uncertainty; it must have faith. History will teach us something of the different results thrown up by these three currents of life. It is hardly necessary to allude to the paralysis of spiritual life that befalls a soul which places itself in the keeping of a church—which surrenders itself to the mortifications and irrational impositions of an irresponsible hierarchy. The abuses, outrages, corruptions, wars, and awful immoralities that have grown out of a church like this, are matters which almost monopolize the pages of history, and sufficiently prove that it has its basis in error and its authority in arrogant assumption. When the people of France pulled down both God and the church, and set up reason in their place, all the infernal elements of human nature held their brief high carnival. That one terrific experiment should be enough for a thousand worlds, through countless years.

So, cut off in all other directions, we come back to the Bible. If that be not authoritative, nothing is. If that be not infallible, as a revelation from God of his own character, the nature of the coming life, and the relations of this life to it, then nothing is infallible, and the faith, without which earth is a cheat and life a sorry jest, is impossible. What do we find to be the fruits of a living, practical faith in an infallible Bible? The most prominent, or that which appears most prominent, in the eyes of the world, is a missionary spirit in contradistinction to a proselyting spirit. The really missionary work of the world has been done in the past, and is now being effected, by those who receive the Bible unmutilated as God's word to men. The noblest heroisms that illustrate the history of the race have their inspiration in implicit faith in the Bible. Men in whom life was fresh and strong, and women who were the impersonations of gentleness and delicacy, have died for it the martyr's death of fire, singing until the red-tongued flames licked up their breath. Out of it have come all pure moralities. Forth from it have sprung all sweet charities. It has been the motive power of regeneration and reformation to millions of men. It has comforted the humble, consoled the mourning, sustained the suffering, and given trust and triumph to the dying. The wise old man has fallen asleep with it folded to his breast. The simple cottager has used it for his dying pillow; and even the innocent child has breathed his last happy sigh with his fingers between its promise-freighted leaves.

Suppose it could be proved that this Bible is all a fable: in what would the demonstration benefit us? It is all we have. If it do not infallibly teach us the truth concerning the future life, and instruct us in the way of making that future life a happy one, then there is nothing that does. Suppose it could be proved that parts of this Bible are fabulous, and that those portions which are not so were inspired in a kind of general way, like the writings of all genius which is both great and good: who would be the better or the happier for it? I believe it to be demonstrable that no greater calamity could befall the human race than either the general loosening up, or the entire destruction, of faith in the Bible, even were the whole of it a cunning invention of the brain of man. Better an ass that carries us than a horse that throws us. Better faith in a fable which inspires to good deeds, conducts our powers to noble ends, makes us loving, gentle, and heroic, eradicates our selfishness, establishes within us the principle of benevolence, and enables us to meet death with equanimity if not with triumph, in the hope of a glorious resurrection and a happy immortality, than the skepticism of a kingly reason, which only needs to be carried to its legitimate issues to bestialize the human race, and drape the earth in the blackness of Tartarus.

So, I say, let us stick to the Bible—the whole of it —from Genesis to Revelation. When the apostle, standing on the heights of inspiration, places the hand of the second Adam in the hand of the first—the Adam of Genesis—I believe there was such an Adam, and that the apostle believed it, and knew it. When I see Christianity emerging naturally and logically from a religion of types and ordinances, I believe that that religion is a portion of the system of divine truth When Christ, standing in the Temple, declares that the Scriptures testify of him, I believe they do thus testify, and that it is right that they be bound up with the Gospels and the Epistles as an essential portion of the grand whole. I find the writers of the New Testament constantly referring to the Old, and the Old prophesying, or recording the preparation for, the events described in the New. There is much that I do not understand, and no little that seems incredible; but I see no leaf that I have either the right or the wish to tear out and cast away. I receive it as, in itself, independent of my reason and my knowledge, an authentic, inspired, and harmonious whole. I pin my faith to it, and rely upon it as the foundation of my own hope and the hope of the world.

Rational minds will ask for no higher proof that the Bible, in its entirety, is reliable as a revelation from God, than the nature of the faith which is based upon it, and the results of that faith—the noblest phenomena of human experience—the consummate fruitage of human civilization. But were it otherwise, the Bible is our best wealth. Were it widely, wildly otherwise, Heaven withhold the hand that would touch it destructively! Crazy Kate, who parted with her sailor boy at the garden gate half a century ago, believes he will come back to her again, carries still in her withered bosom the keepsake which he gave her, and decks her silvery hair and her little room with flowers, to give him fitting welcome. This hope is her all. In this she lives; and in this, fallacious though it be, resides all the significance of her life. As she stands upon the rock worn smooth by her constant feet, and gazes hopefully across the saddening sea into the yellow sunset, to catch a glimpse of the long-expected sail, would it not be inhuman to plunder her of the keepsake and toss it into the waves, or tear from her the hope that fills with blood and breath the long perished object of her idolatry, and swells the phantom sails that are winging him to her bosom? Whether true or false, the Bible is our all—the one regenerative, redemptive agency in the world—the only word that even sounds as if it came from the other side of the wave. If we lose it, we are lost.

III.

PATIENCE.

"The world was not made in a minute."
"Every thing comes in time to him who can wait."
"For all one's early rising it dawns none the sooner."
"What ripens fast does not last," or, "soon ripe, soon rotten."

IF there be one attribute of the Deity which astonishes me more than another, it is the attribute of patience. The Great Soul that sits on the throne of the universe is not, never was, and never will be, in a hurry. In the realm of nature, every thing has been wrought out in the august consciousness of infinite leisure; and I bless God for that geology which gives me a key to the patience in which the creative process was effected. Man has but a brief history. A line of nineteen old men, centenarians, would, if they were to join hands, clasp the hand of Christ; and the sixtieth of such a line would tell us that his name is Adam, and that he does not know who his mother was. Yet this wonderful earth, unquestionably constructed with reference to the accommodation of our race, was begun so long ago that none but fools undertake to reckon its age by the measurement of years. Ah! what baths of fire and floods of water; what earthquakes, eruptions, upheavals, and storms; what rise and fall of vegetable and animal dispensations; what melting and moulding and combining of elements, have been patiently gone through with, to fit up this dwelling-place of man! When I look back upon the misty surface of the dimly retiring ages—the smoking track over which the train of creative change has swept—it fades until the sky of the past eternity shuts down upon the vision; and I only know that far beyond that point—infinitely far—that train commenced its progress, and that, even then, God only opened his hand to give flight to a thought that He had held imprisoned from eternity!

But the old rocks tell us that there was a time when animal life began—rude and rudimentary; typical and prophetic, the geologists say. We may call it typical and prophetic, if we choose; and, in a sense, it undoubtedly is so. But, to me, all these forms of animal life are simply patient studies of man. There seem to be parts of man in every thing that went before him. As I find in the studio of the artist who has completed a great picture, studies of heads and hands, and limbs and scenes which the picture embodies—convenient prisons of fleeting ideas—experiments in composition and effect—so do I find in the records of pre-Adamic life only a succession of studies having reference to the great picture of humanity. God was in no haste to get the world ready for man, and in no haste to make him. There was coal to lay up in exhaustless storehouses. There were continents to be upheaved, seas to chain, river-channels to carve. There was an infinite variety of germs to be invented and made in heaven, a soil to be prepared for their reception on the earth's surface, and a broadcast sowing to be effected. What infinite detail! What intimate arrangement of special laws that should not clash with one another! How could the Creator wait so long to see the being for whom all this pains-taking preparation was in progress?

Well, when the process was at last completed; when the marvellously beautiful but diminutive form of Adam walked out of God's thought into the morning sunlight of Eden—walked through flowers and odors, and among animals that licked his hand and gambolled around him unscared; when the impalpable forms of angels were thick around him in an atmosphere uneasy with its burden of vitality, how did the Creator regard him—the object of all this patient working and waiting? It was what we should call "a great success."

It was "very popular" with the observing host. The morning stars sang together, and all the sons of God shouted for joy; but God did not even say that it was "very good;" He only "saw" that it was so. No ruffle of exultation swept over the bosom of that sublime patience, for even then he had only made a beginning! He had only made a place for his creatures to dwell in. Before Him stretched almost infinite cycles of duration. In the far perspective, He saw nations rise and sink, civilizations blossom and decay, the advent and the mission of Jesus, the struggles of good and evil, of light and darkness, of truth and error; and on the remote pinnacle of destiny, faintly rising to his eye in the eternity before him, the blazing windows and the white pillars and spires of the Temple of Consummation!

Some people wonder how God can bear as He does with human frailty and wickedness. In effect, they ask why He does not sweep the whole race out of existence, and start again. As if the Being who had patiently wrought and waited for myriads of ages to prepare for man had not patience to allow him to work out his destiny! Ah, short-sighted mortals! Has not God an eternity to accomplish His ends in? Is He, before the eyes of a universe, to relinquish an experiment, and pronounce that to be a failure on which He has expended such infinite pains and patience? Not

He; and the man must be idiotic who cannot draw from this patience food for hope, even when mercy seems exhausted.

But this divine element enters more or less into human character, and it is with this that we have specially to do. There is no well-doing—no godlike doing—that is not patient doing. There is no great achievement that is not the result of patient working and waiting. There is no royal road to any thing. One thing at a time—all things in succession. That which grows fast, withers as rapidly; that which grows slowly, endures. The silver-leafed poplar grows in one decade, and dies in the next; the oak takes its century to grow in, and lives and dies at leisure. This law runs through all vegetation, through all creation, and through all human achievement. A fortune won in a day is lost in a day; a fortune won slowly, and slowly compacted, seems to acquire from the hand that won it the property of endurance. We all see this, we all acknowledge it, yet we are all in a hurry. We are in haste for position; we are in haste for wealth; we are in haste for fame; we are in haste for every thing that is desirable, and that shapes itself into an object of life. In that worthiest of all struggles—the struggle for self-mastery and goodness—we are far less patient with ourselves than God is with us. We forget, too, in our impatience with others—with their weakness and wrong-doing—that there is One who sees this weakness and wickedness as we never can see it, yet is unruffled by it. "Work and wait"—"work and wait"—is what God says to us in Creation and in Providence. We work, and that is godlike; we get impatient, and there crops out our human weakness.

Man of business, do the gains come in slowly? Do your neighbors outstrip you in prosperity? Do you hear of friends grown suddenly rich by great speculations, and is your heart discouraged with the prospect before you? Does it seem to you that your lot is hard beyond that of other men? God is only trying to see how much you are like Him—how much of His own life is in you. If He is the kind father I take Him to be, He is quite as anxious to bless you as you are anxious to be blest; and as He does not appear to be in a hurry to have you become rich, it strikes me that it would be quite as well for you to take your stand with Him, and be willing to work and wait. Don't be in a hurry. The world was not made in a minute; yet what a marvel of beauty and wealth it is! You say that you have worked hard enough, and that is very well; but have you done that which is harder than work, and quite as essential—have you waited patiently and well? Have you not been fretting and complaining all the time? All things come in time to him who can wait.

Weary mother, with a clamorous family at your knee—a family clamorous for bread, for clothing, for amusement, for change for their restless natures—do you get impatient; and do the fretful words sometimes escape to wound those young ears and chafe those fresh hearts? Do you look forward through ten, fifteen, or twenty years, and, seeing no intermission of daily care for these impulsive spirits, and ceaseless ministry to their fickle impulses, sigh over your bondage? Be patient. Think of God's patience with His family—a thousand millions here on the earth alone—deadly quarrels going on among them all the time, cheating between brethren, wildness with greed for gold, millions of them never looking up to thank the hand that feeds them during their life! Think how He looks down, and sees millions bound in compulsory servitude to other millions—sees great multitudes meet in the madness of war to slaughter one another; sees a whole world lying in wickedness, carelessness, and ingratitude. Mark how He causes the seasons to come and go, how seed-time and harvest fail not, how His unwearied servant the sun shines on the evil and the good alike, how the gentle rain falls with no discrimination on the just and the unjust. Think how He patiently bears with your impatience. Listen! There comes no outcry from the heavens to still all this wild unrest; but gently, patiently, the ministry of nature and of Providence proceeds from day to day and from year to year—as gently and patiently and unremittingly, as if it were universally greeted with gratitude, and nourished only plants that were blossoming with praise. Can you not be patient with the little ones you love for a little while? You really ought to be ashamed of impatience, with such an example of patience as God gives, especially as you are a sharer in its benefits.

Discouraged pastor, mourning over the lack of results in your ministry, do you sometimes get impatient with the listlessness and coldness of your flock, and rail at them in good set terms? Surely you have forgotten who and what you are. You are God's minister—the promulgator of his religion. He sent the Great Teacher to the earth eighteen hundred years ago: and those to whom He was sent maligned Him, doubted Him, persecuted and killed Him. For eighteen hundred years He has patiently waited to see the religion of Jesus established in the earth, and he is waiting patiently still, though it spreads so slowly that its progress from century to century can hardly be traced. He planted the true seed, and He is confident that it will germinate and grow, until its branches shall fill the whole earth. He has confidence in His truth: have you? Can you not be content, like Him, to plant, and nourish, and water, and tenderly prune, and trust for the issue? He has distinctly told you that with all your planting and watering the increase is only of Him. If you are faithful in these offices, and get impatient for results, does it not occur to you that you are getting quite as impatient with God as you are with your people? If He have reason for withholding increase, you have no reason to find fault. The work is His, the results are His—they are not yours. Therefore be content to work and wait, for no man can work in perfect harmony with God who is not as willing to wait as to work. God works and waits always, and in every thing, and you are a discord in the economy of His universal scheme the moment you become impatient.

Champion of Truth, lover of humanity, hater of wrong, do you grow tired and disgusted with your fellows? Do you grow angry when you contemplate instituted cruelty? Are you tempted to turn your back upon those whom you have striven to bless, when they stop their ears, or laugh you in the face? Do you feel your spirit stirred with deep disgust, or swelling with rage, when those to whom you have given your best life—your noblest love, your most humane impulses, your truest ideal of that which is good—contemn you, misconstrue you, and persecute you;—when those whom you seek to reform brand you as a pestilent fellow, a disturber, and a busybody? It is very natural that you should do so, but it is far from godlike. Be patient. If this world of natural beauty was not made in a minute; if it had to go through convulsions and changes, age after age, before the flowers could grow and the maize could spring, think you that the little drop of vital power that is in you can reform the world of mind, and bring out of chaos the realization of the fair ideal that is in you in the brief space of your life? Pour into your age your whole life, if it be pure and good, and be sure that you have done something—your little all. There shall be no drop of that life wasted. Where you put it there it shall be, an atom in the slowly rising monument of a world redeemed to goodness.

If you cannot take counsel of God in this thing, and, with the counsel, courage, take it from the most insignificant of His creatures—the madrepores that build islands covered with gardens of wonderful beauty under the sea. The little polyp may well be discouraged when it sees how little it can do in the creation of the coral world to which, by a law of its nature, it is bound to contribute. But it gives to this world the entire results of its little life—a calcareous atom—and then it dies. But that atom is not lost; God takes care of that. All He asks of the madrepore is its life, and though it may not witness the glory of the structure it assists to rear, it has a place in the structure—an essential place—and there it is glorified. Through those strangely-fashioned trees the green sea sweeps.

and wondering monsters swim and stare, till, little by little, as the ages with heavy feet tramp over the upper earth, they rear themselves into the light, and hold the turbulent sea asleep beneath the smile of God. Little by little they lay the foundations upon which a new life rests, and become the eternal pillars of a temple in which man worships, and from which his voice of praise ascends to Heaven. Therefore, if the patience of God do not inspire and instruct you, let the self-sacrifice of the polyp shame you, and the results of that sacrifice encourage you. Give that little life of yours with its little result to the twig where you hang, never minding the surges of the sea that try to dislodge you, nor the monsters that stare at you, and be sure that the tree shall emerge at last into the light of Heaven—the basis and the assurance of a new and glorious life for a race.

Poet, forger of ideals, dreamer among the possibilities of life, prophet of the millennium, do you get impatient with the prosaic life around you—the dulness, and the earthliness, and the brutishness of men? Fret not. Go forward into the realm which stretches before you; climb the highest mountain you can reach, and plant a cross there. The nations will come up to it some day. Work for immortality if you will; then wait for it. If your own age fail to recognize you, a coming age will not. Plunge into the eternal forest that sleeps in front, and blaze the trees. Be a pioneer of Time's armies as they march into the unseen and unknown. Signalize the advance guard from afar. If you have the privilege of living the glorious life of which you dream, are you not paid? Why, there are uncounted multitudes who walk under the stars, and never dream that they are beautiful. There are crowds who trample a flower into the dust, without once thinking that they have one of the sweetest thoughts of God under their heel. There are myriads of stolid eyes that gaze into the ethereal vermilion of a sunset without dreaming that God lighted the fire. The world could see no beauty in the greatest life and character that ever existed, why they should desire it, and yet God does not get impatient because He is not recognized. The stars stud the sky as thickly as ever; the flowers bloom as freshly as at first, and breathe no complaints with their dying perfume; the sunset patiently varies its picture from nightfall to nightfall, though no one praises it; and Christ, in the garb of humble men and women, looks from pure and patient eyes in every street, and ooks none the less sweetly because he is not seen. Therefore, O poet, be patient, though the world see not the visions that enchain you, and remember what companionship is yours. Aye, be patient!

IV.

PERFECT LIBERTY.

"For the upright there are no laws."
"Laws were made for rogues."
"Love rules his kingdom without a sword."
"Love makes labor light."

A TIPSY man, laboring alike under an uncomfortable confusion of ideas and an incompetent control of his muscles, is apt to find a sidewalk of common width too narrow for him. The trees and lamp-posts rush with violence to assault him, curbstones rise in his path with ruffianly greetings, and the inclination of a dead level is such that at last he slides into the gutter, where he breathes out his curses upon the dangers of the way. The sober man walks the same path without seeing lamp-post or tree, and without being conscious of the slightest restraint upon his movements. We put a poke upon a vicious cow, because she has a disposition to go precisely where she is not wanted to go—into a cornfield, where she will do serious damage to the proprietor, and kill herself with over-eating. She comes up to the fence that she would fain demolish or surmount, and the new restraint vexes her beyond measure. Her companion in the field is an innocent, docile creature, that is content with her honest grass, and her honest way of getting it. So, while the thief stands raving and floundering at the fence, she fills herself with clover, and contentedly lies down to the pleasant task of rumination, without a thought of restraint or deprivation. For the innocent cow there is no poke.

The perfect liberty of any faculty of the mind lies within the range of its office. Acquisitiveness is a faculty of mind. It is endowed with a certain legitimate office, and in that office it has full liberty—liberty in the field in which it has its life. If it overstep the bound of its office, and steal, it preys upon the fruits of the liberty of others, and degenerates into licentiousness. Then it feels the law which defines the boundaries of its field of liberty, but until that time, the law is a thing unfelt. A horse, standing upon the beach, and looking out to the sea as a realm forbidden to him, may be imagined to find fault with the line of surf that warns him away from a region in which he has no legitimate rights and no legitimate office. The beach may be free to him for miles, and pastures may recede from it for other miles, over which he has liberty to run and range at will, with the opportunity to supply all his wants, and expend all his vitality. If he plunge into the sea, he feels the law that defines the boundaries of his perfect liberty. Laws are the very bulwarks of liberty. They define every man's rights, and stand between and defend the individual liberties of all men. The moment that law is destroyed, liberty is lost; and men left free to enter upon the domains of each other, destroy each other's rights, and invade the field of each other's liberty.

No man ever feels the restraint of law so long as he remains within the sphere of his liberty—a sphere, by the way, always large enough for the full exercise of his powers and the supply of all his legitimate wants. It is only rogues who feel the restraints of law. We live in a free country, and its freedom consists in the protection which the laws give to each man's liberty to pursue his legitimate ends of life in a legitimate way. We rejoice in these laws, because they guard our liberty—not because they interfere with it. We make them, support them, and obey them, in the exercise of our liberty. They stand between us and that licentiousness which is the invader and destroyer of liberty. There is no state of society under heaven, and there can be none, where perfect liberty exists, without an obedience to law so glad and so entire that the restraints of the law are unfelt.

Thus much is true, without any reference to God, or any relation to religion. Thus much is philosophically true. Advancing a step in the discussion, another element enters in—the element of love—the perfect law of liberty. The moment the soul is lifted in love to its Maker, and extended in love to its fellows, the whole realm of law is illuminated by a new light, and there is only darkness beyond its boundaries. Before this illumination, self-interest, or right philosophical judgment may be sufficient to keep the soul contentedly within the boundaries of law. After it, it becomes the subject of duty—duty to God and duty to man. It recognizes relationships on the lines of which it is to flow out in piety and good works. The law which defines its individual liberty is in a measure sunk out of sight, and the law which defines its duty is that only which it sees. The influx of this new love is essentially the influx of a new life. This realm of duty is the one which, through the vestibule of law, I have endeavored to lead the reader.

Can the soul enjoy perfect liberty in the realm of duty? This question I wish to answer for the benefit of a great multitude of men and women who, with a sense of great self-sacrifice, have taken upon them the responsibilities of the Christian life. To these, this life is a life of crosses and mortifications. They find their duty unpleasant and onerous. It is to them a law of restraint and constraint. They are constantly oppressed with what they denominate "a sense of duty." It torments them with a consciousness of their inefficiency, with a painful and persistent questioning of their motives, with multiplied and perplexing doubts of the genuineness of their religious experience. Christian liberty is a phrase of which they know not the meaning, for they are, in fact and in feeling, the slaves of duty. They feel themselves enchained within the bounds of a system superinduced upon their life, and not in any proper sense incorporated with it.

I ask the question again: Can the soul enjoy perfect liberty in the realm of duty? I answer in the affirmative, and express my belief that that liberty may be of as much higher quality and of as much greater extent than in the realm of pure law, as the love from which it springs is superior as a basis of action to an intellectual apprehension and acceptation of law as the condition of liberty. Love is its own law, and duty is only the name of those lines of action which naturally flow out from love. I apprehend nothing as Christian duty which does not naturally flow out from Christian love. All those actions which love naturally dictates and performs, if performed by any individual as simple duties—performed grudgingly and difficultly—amount to nothing as Christian actions. They become simply bald acts of morality, and have no connection with religion. Let me not be misunderstood. Love may constrain to acts that, for various reasons, are difficult of performance ; but difficult acts, performed from a simple sense of duty—acts in no way growing out of love—acts performed only for the satisfaction of conscience and for the acquisition of mental peace—are not Christian acts, essentially, and cannot be made to appear such.

Love, I say again, is its own law. A man who loves God supremely, and his neighbor as himself, may do exactly what he pleases—all that he wishes to do—all that by this love he is moved to do. There is no license here, for a man possessed by these affections will please to do, wish to do, and be moved to do, only those things that follow the lines of duty. Here is Christian liberty, and it is nowhere else. Here is Christian liberty, and there is no such other liberty as this under the sun. It is the liberty of angels and of God Himself. It rises infinitely above the liberty defined by law, and is, in fact and in terms, "the liberty of the sons of God"—one of the most suggestive and inspiriting phrases, by the way, contained within the lids of the Bible. The most beautiful sight this earth affords is a man or woman so filled with love that duty is only a name, and its performance the natural outflow and expression of the love which has become the central principle of their life. For such men and women there is neither law nor duty, as a hinderance to perfect liberty. They are on a plane above both. They live essentially in the same love out of which law and duty proceeded. Law and duty were born of love. Love originally drew their outlines and carved the channels of their operation, and, rising into an appropriation and incorporation of the mother element, the soul loses, of course, the necessity of its offspring,—has, in fact, within itself both element and offspring.

Perhaps my meaning will be more exactly apprehended by the use of illustrations. A woman finds herself the mother of a family of children, whom she loves as her own life. It is against the law that she turn them out of doors, or kill them, or maltreat them in any way. Does she feel the restraint of these laws? Does she ever think of their existence? Do they curtail her liberty to any extent? Not at all, for her love is her law. Rising now into the realm of duty, we see that she owes to them the preparation of their food, the care of their persons and clothing, ministry in sickness, home education, sympathy in trouble, discipline for disobedience, and all motherly offices. Now do these duties come to her simply as duties? Does she feed and clothe her children, minister to them in sickness, educate them and sympathize with them, from a sense of duty? Ah, no! In the domain of motherly duty, love is her law, and the performance of these duties is simply the natural outflow and expression of the love which she bears to her children. The stronger and the more perfect her love, the smaller the restraints of law and the constraints of duty; and when this love becomes, as in many instances it does become, an all-absorbing passion, law and duty, in connection with her relations to her children, are things she never even dreams of. Her neighbors may call her a slave to her children, but she knows that she is in the enjoyment of a most delicious liberty—the liberty to do precisely those things which please her most, inspired by a love that knows neither law nor duty.

Suppose now that this mother die and a step-mother take her place. She may find among those children one so intractable and ungrateful that it would be a pleasure to her to turn it out of the house, but the law prevents. She then looks upon law as a restraint upon her liberty. But, in the place she has taken, she perceives that she owes duties to this family of children. She has an intellectual appreciation of the duties of her office, and undertakes to perform them. We will suppose that, from a simple sense of duty, she devotes herself to them as thoroughly as their own mother did before her. Under circumstances like these, duty would become a burden, and a bondage. What was almost a divine liberty with the mother, becomes to the step-mother a crushing slavery. Conscientious but unloving, she wears out a life of servitude to duty, and of course is most unhappy.

It seems to me that these simple illustrations throw unmistakable light upon this whole subject. Christian love knows no such thing as slavery to law and to duty The higher, the purer, and the stronger this love, the more do law and duty disappear, until, finally, they are unthought of, and the soul finds itself free—without a single shackle on its faculties, or a single restraint upon its movements. It acts within the lines of law, because its highest life naturally lives within them. Those lines are not described to it by a foreign or superior power; they are defined by itself, in the full exercise of liberty born of love. It performs its duties because they lie in the path of its natural action. Neither restraint nor constraint is felt, because, in the perfect liberty which is born of perfect love, it chooses to do, and does, that against which there is no law, and that in which abides all duty.

So, if there be any struggling, sorrowful Christians, who are in the habit of taking up daily crosses, and doing unpleasant things, because, and simply because, they deem them to be duties, I have only this to say to them—that no act of theirs, performed simply because it is a duty, and performed with a sense of constraint that does not come from genuine love to God and man, can be looked back upon as a Christian duty worthily performed. As a moral act, conscientiously performed, there is in it a quality of goodness, but it is the work of a slave and not of a freeman. My servant may bring me a glass of water because I command her to, and in so doing she will perform her duty, though it may be to her a task. If, when I enter my house, heated with walking and labor, my daughter bring me a glass of water, from love of me and sympathy for me, the character of the act is essentially changed. Her act is in the domain of perfect liberty, and had its birth in love. The two acts are identical, they cost the same amount of labor, both were performed in the discharge of a duty, yet the dullest intellect will apprehend a difference in their quality that elevates one almost infinitely above the other.

There is no release in this world, or the next, from the restraints of law and the constraints of duty, save in love. Duty, especially out of the domain of love, is the veriest slavery of the world. The cry of the soul is for freedom. It longs for liberty, from the date of its first conscious moments. This natural longing is not born of depravity, but points with an unerring finger to a source of satisfaction existing somewhere for it in the universe of God. Law surrounds us while we are low, and we beat our heads against it and are baffled. Duty takes us upon a higher plane—on the plane of conscience, or an insufficient Christian love, and forces us to the performance of tasks which are hard and ungrateful. We ask for something better than this, and we get it when love fills us full of itself, and absorbs us into itself. What the Christian world wants is more love. Love rules his kingdom without a sword. There is no compulsion here. Love makes labor light. There are no unpleasant tasks here—at least, none whose unpleasantness destroys a divine pleasure in their performance. A man who feels that his religion is a slavery, has not begun to comprehend the real nature of religion. That heart of his is still selfish. There is lacking the elevation, the entire consecration which alone can introduce him into that glorious liberty which the real sons of God enjoy.

Ah, this liberty! How little have we of it in the world! How we go groping, and mourning, and wailing through the darkness—walled in by law, goaded on by duty, and filled with the fears which perfect love casts out, when all the while there hang above us crowns within our reach, which, grasped, would make us kings! Oh, it is very pitiful—this sight of Christian slaves! Most pitiful, however, does it become, when we comprehend the fact that in this slavery many think they find the evidence of their Christianity. They bear burdens throughout their lives which wear into their very hearts, and think there is merit in it. Mortification, penance, bondage—are these the rewards of

Christianity? Crosses, servitude, fear—are these the credentials of love? Out upon such mischievous error! Into it, God forbid that soul of yours or mine should be drawn! What great wonder is it that the world is frightened away from such bondage as this?

No: perfect love holds the secret of the world's perfect liberty. It is only this that releases us from law, and discharges us from duty, by making law the definition of our life, and duty the natural, free outflow of our souls. Into this liberty Divine Love would lead us. Up to it would Heaven lift us. In it only is the perfection of Christian action. In it only can the soul find that freedom for which it has yearned through all its history. In it only lives an exuberant, boundless joy—joy in tribulation, joy in labor, joy in every thing except that world of slavish life that lives below it, bound to law and duty, to forms and creeds, to mortifications and penances, selfishness and sin. We shall know more about it up yonder.

V.

TRUST, AND WHAT COMES OF IT.

"He who sows his land trusts in God."
"Trust everybody, but thyself most."
"Trusting often makes fidelity."
"If you would make a thief honest, trust him."
"Trust thyself only, and another shall not betray thee."

IT is sadly humiliating to think that more than a moiety of the world's trust in God is blind and unconscious. We trust in lines of precedent, and links of succession, and laws and principles. Very little of our trust is immediate.. We sow our seed, and bury it in the earth, trusting that the germs we deposit will proceed to the beautiful unfolding of the harvest; yet our trust is in the seed, the season, the sun, the soil—any thing but the God who instituted vegetable life, and all its laws and conditions. We are compelled to trust something, however, or we should die. Trust lies at the basis of every scheme of human life, and is the corner-stone of the temple of human happiness. If our trust fail to reach God directly, or if it fail to become transitive through nature into God, then it must abide in nature. It must live somewhere. We trust to some power or principle for the rising and the setting of the sun, for the sleep of winter, the resurrection of spring, the fructification of summer, and the fruition of autumn. We know nothing of the future. We do not know that rain will fall—that seed-time and harvest will come; but we trust that they will; and this trust is so strong that, practically, it answers the purposes of foreknowledge—it brings the feeling of security to the heart, and furnishes a basis for the plans necessary to perpetuate the life of the race. But we trust no further than we can see. Something must come between us and the Being upon whom we rely for every thing, before our hearts will poise themselves in trust. We trust nature, our fellows, and even God Himself, because we are obliged to. We would trust nobody and no thing if we could get along without it. We trust nature because, if we did not, we could not live. We trust God, strongly or feebly, because we know that in the life beyond this our destiny is in His hands. We trust our fellows, because it is necessary to have one heart, at least, in whose confidence we may dwell. A man who is poor in trust is the poorest of all God's creatures.

Now why this strange reluctance in trusting? Why should it be necessary to force us into trusting when, without it, we cannot be happy for a moment—when, without it, we cannot institute a single plan relating to the future? I think that the lack of trust in God and our universal distrust of men grow out of a sense of our own ill desert and our own untrustworthiness. I find always those who are the richest in trust toward God and man the most trustworthy in themselves. I find those who go about with open hearts and honest lips, with no intent of evil toward others, those who trust men the most invariably. The child trusts because it finds no reason in itself why it should not. The charity that thinketh no evil trusts in God and trusts in men. The heart that knows itself to be false, trusts neither in God nor men. So, naturally, and after the common order of things, we shall get no more trust in this world until the world which must bring the grace into exercise is better. As this world grows better, the trust which forms the basis of its happiness will grow broader, a more luxuriant social life will spring up, and the great brotherhood of humanity will not only come nearer together, but they will be blended and fused in an all-pervading sympathy.

Naturally, and after the common order of things, I say, the world will have no more voluntary trust until it is better; but trusting as a policy may be instituted for the purpose of making the world better, and it is this policy that I propose to make the subject of this article. A child that comes to me in danger, or sorrow, or perplexity, and takes my hand, and looks into my eyes, and utters its wants in trust, begets in me trustworthiness, on the instant. It rouses into action all within me that is good and honorable and true, and I cannot betray that trust without a loss of self-respect that will make me contemn myself for a life-time. A maiden who comes into my presence in guileless trust, and in any way places her destiny in my hands, would shame me into trustworthiness were my heart teeming with impurity. Even the timid hare, hunted from field to field, and hard beset by the baying hounds, would find a protector in me should it leap desperately into my arms, and lay the tumult of its frightened heart upon the generous beatings of mine. The child, the maiden, the hare would beget in me trustworthiness, simply by trusting me. They would make me considerate and generous and honorable. I should despise myself were I to harm either by a thought. uch beings, under such circumstances, would come to me as missionaries, bearing one of the very sweetest of the lessons of Christ.

These illustrations seem to me to be pregnant with meaning, and instinct with illumination. They open to me the door of a policy, and reveal to me a ministry equally beautiful and beneficent, yet they involve no new law, and spring out of no newly-discovered princi ple. All seed produces after its kind. If I plant corn, I reap corn; if I plant lilies, I gather lilies. Like produces like in the spiritual no less than in the material universe. Love begets love; anger begets anger. If I sow to the wind, I reap the whirlwind. So, if I sow trust, I reap trust. The soil will honor the seed. Of course, I state this as a general fact. There are souls as well as soils that will produce nothing good. There are souls as well as soils so sour, so rank with pollution, or so poor, that nothing but weeds will grow in them; but, as a general fact, in the worlds of mind and matter, the soil will honor the seed. Wherever there may be the slightest promise of return, we are to sow our trust.

Now what is the aspect that life presents to us? Is it not that of universal distrust? Nay, has not distrust become an instituted thing, that has taken form in maxims and proverbs? There is hardly a language that does not contain a proverb which says in words, or effect, "Trust thyself only, and another shall not betray thee"—a proverb that bears the very singe and scent of hell. Thus distrust is not only a fact, but it has become a policy. It is inculcated by universal human society; and as like produces like, distrust is everywhere reaped, because it is everywhere sown.

We take no pains to nurse honor by trusting it. We trust interest and appetite, and every thing base and selfish in a man, quicker than we do any good quality in him. We trust that which is beast-like in men, and refuse to trust that which is godlike. We decline to bring honor into exercise, and honor dwindles under the treatment.

One of the most notable illustrations of the evil consequences of distrust is that afforded by the relative positions of the sexes. The institutions of society and education, so far as they have to do with these relations, are established on the theory that men and women are not to be trusted together. Our colleges and schools, and all the institutions and usages of social life, recognize, as a cardinal fact, the untrustworthiness of men and women. They proceed upon the theory that men will betray if they can, and that virtue in women is only a name. Wherever this theory is pushed to its extreme, there we shall find always the qualities suspected. I suppose that there is no country in the world where young women are guarded with such care as in France. The very extreme of punctilio is exacted on the part of parents, and a woman is hardly allowed to see her lover alone until after her marriage. The duenna is her companion in society, as constantly as her own shadow. Yet in France, as in all countries where this extreme of caution is observed—where this distrust takes its severest form—is female virtue the rarest, and masculine licentiousness the most universal. Virtue shrinks and refuses to live in the atmosphere of universal distrust. Manly purity and honor find no use for themselves where they are neither believed in nor appealed to. This distrust of the sexes, so persistently and powerfully inculcated by society, breeds untrustworthiness, and sows broadcast the seeds of impurity. It always has been so, and it always will be. There is no remedy but in releasing society from the control of men and women who are sadly conscious of their own weaknesses, and in the assumption of the functions of education by men who are something more than saintly and suspicious grandmothers.

Just look at this thing. Here are two sexes, intended by Heaven to be the companions of each other—intended to ennoble and purify each other, to enter into the most intimate, endearing and permanent relations with each other, to draw from each other the very choicest of their earthly happiness—the two hemispheres of humanity necessary to the perfection and beauty of the great sphere of life—yet trained from the first dawning of their regard for one another to believe in their mutual untrustworthiness They are seated on different sides of the room where they meet to worship a common Lord. They are caged in boarding-schools, kept from association by all possible means, kept as much as may be from all knowledge of each other, trained to impurity of imagination by the very restraints which are put upon them to keep them pure. I believe in manly honor and womanly virtue; and that the more we trust them the more we develop them. I believe that an honor never developed by the trust of pure and womanly hearts, and a virtue that has always lived in the poisonous atmosphere of distrust, and has never come out to stand alone in its own sweet self-assertion, are as good as brown paper, and only better in exceptional instances. I believe that all that is needed in America to make our nation as untrustworthy as France, is to draw the reins still tighter, build the walls of partition still higher, and come up, or down, to the policy of ignoring or contemning any power of virtue in men and women that will keep them from sin.

Now let us take a very simple and suggestive illustration of this principle of trust as it bears upon our general life. We meet, passing through the streets of the city or town where we live, a stranger. He approaches us, and informs us that he has lost his way, and inquires the direction of his lodgings. He places himself, in his ignorance and helplessness, in our hands. He trusts the direction of his footsteps entirely to us. We can deceive him if we will; but we are upon our honor at once. We are trusted, and our hearts spring naturally and instantaneously up to honor that trust. Now there is not one man in one hundred, in any class of society, who will not honor so simple a trust, and who does not feel that he is happier and better in consequence of honoring it. As polite and hearty offices of kindness has it been my lot to receive from entire strangers, under circumstances like these, as I have ever received in my life. To my mind, this little illustration denotes the general trustworthiness of men, and shows to me that if I approach my fellows in a simple, honest trust, they will deal fairly with me. Perhaps I should except itinerant dealers in crockery and glassware, professional Peter Funks, Irishmen who work by the job, and others whose sole living it is to get large returns for insignificant investments. But I do not propose to deal with these. They are not my fellows, and I have no relations with them.

Everything good in a man thrives best when properly recognized. Men do about what we expect of them. If a man with whom I have business relations perceive that I expect him to cheat me if he can, he will commonly do it. If, on the contrary, he see that I place implicit faith in his honor—that I trust him—every thing good in the man springs into life, and demands that that trust be honored. The sordid elements of his character may possibly triumph, but they will triumph by a struggle which will weaken them.

If I am unwilling to trust my son or my daughter out of my sight, I may reasonably expect to plant and nourish in them precisely those qualities which would make it dangerous for them to be out of my sight. If I refuse to trust the word of an honest man, I may reasonably expect that with me, at least, he will break faith at the earliest opportunity. If I place all men and women at arm's length, in the fear that one of them will be treacherous to me, I place myself beyond the desert of good treatment at their hands—beyond the reach of their sympathies and their good-will—in short, I insult them, and voluntarily institute an antagonism which naturally breeds mischief in them toward me.

So I advocate the policy of universal faith, as an essential condition of universal faithfulness—of universal trust as a pre-requisite for universal trustworthiness. The world does not half comprehend the principle of overcoming evil with good, but clings to the infernal policy of overcoming evil with evil. I know of no power in the world but good, with which to overcome evil; and when I see on every side exhibitions of a ack of personal honor, I know that I can foster the honor that remains in no way except by recognizing it and calling it into development by direct practical appeal. One of the most remarkable and suggestive passages in the Bible, as it seems to me, is this:—"If we love not our brother whom we have seen, how can we love God, whom we have not seen?" Many will fail to see how such a conclusion naturally follows from such premises; but a little consideration will show that by the amount in which godlike elements enter into humanity, do human elements enter into divinity; and that if we fail to recognize and love these elements as they are exhibited to us in human life, we shall necessarily fail to recognize and love the same elements in a Being removed beyond our vision, and, save as we see Him in humanity, beyond our comprehension. Now this thing is just as true of trust as it is of love. If we fail to trust that which is good in our brother, whom we have seen, how can we trust the same qualities in a Being whom we have not seen, and of whom we know nothing definitely, save as He has exhibited Himself to us in human life? I know of nothing that antagonizes more directly with trust in the divine Being than the attitude and habit of distrust which we maintain towards our fellows. I believe that history and observation will prove the entire soundness of this principle, and will show that every soul that sits apart from its brotherhood, in settled distrust, is devoid of faith and trust in the Being from whom it sprang. I believe that God has laid the way to trust in Himself through humanity, and that those who refuse to walk in it will fail to find a short cut to Him.

Trust in man, then, is not only the true policy for

the development of trustworthiness in man, but it is the legitimate path over which we must walk to the attainment of a secure and happy piety. Let us then throw the door of our hearts wide open. Let us give our hand to our brother in honest trust. One may possibly abuse our trust; but ninety-nine in one hundred will not; and we cannot afford to sacrifice so great a good for ourselves, and the great mass of men, to save our confidence from a single betrayal. We do not refuse our dirty pence to a beggar who appears to be in need, because he may abuse the gift; but we say that it is better that ten betray our trust than that one innocent man should suffer want. When the universal heart longs for trust, delights in trust, is made better by trust, and needs trust, we should give so cheap a thing freely. Especially should we do it when we can legitimately apply those precious words to the gift—"Inasmuch as ye did it unto the least of these, ye did it unto me."

VI.

THE IDEAL CHRIST.

"Like master, like man."

IDEALS are the world's masters. That self which thinks, and judges, and knows, is always in advance of that other self which wills, and acts, and lives; and all the spare capital of the soul—all that is not appropriated to the daily uses and experiences of its life—is invested in ideals—projected into forms where it may be kept, contemplated, and worshipped, as the instituted sources of its inspiration. That which is godlike in men goes ahead of them into some form of their own choosing, to beckon them toward perfection and to lead them toward God. Wherever our affections cluster, there springs up an ideal character. Our ideal may not be up to the character which serves as its nucleus, nor identical with it in any way; but, wherever God sees our love concentrating, He plants himself in the form of our noblest conceptions of honor, purity, and goodness, that we may be attracted towards Him. We follow the lines of the flight of our conceptions as the bee-hunters follow the flight of bees, for a little distance, and then we pause and let them feed again at our hearts, and follow their flight again, and repeat the process till, deep in the heart of the tree of life, we discover the store-house of the Divine Sweetness. God uses the ideals that we build as the media through which He inspires us. He employs them as agents by which to mould our character, so that if we could know the precise form of a man's ideals, we could know the influences at work upon him for his elevation and purification.

To illustrate the fact that our ideals are framed upon the objects of our affections, or the subjects of our nobler sentiments, and that all their inspiring influences come to us on the lines of these affections and sentiments, let me suppose an instance of the passion of love between the sexes. A man makes the acquaintance of a woman who inspires him with love. His reason, and all his previous knowledge of women, tell him that she is imperfect. His friends may tell him that she has a bad temper, that she is weak, that she is vain. But his love is fixed, and is as strong as a passion can be that lives in his nature; and his imagination springs to clothe her with all human perfections. Her movements are poetry, her eye is heaven, her voice is music, and her presence that of an angel. To him she is a pure, exalted, and beautiful being, and he worships the quali ties with which he invests her. Now it is very evident that he does not love the woman herself, but his ideal—the creation of his own mind—the embodiment of his highest ideas of womanly loveliness.

Mark how this ideal becomes an active power upon him—how it works a miracle upon him. Impure thoughts are banished from his mind, all inferior and unworthy aims are forsaken, he withdraws himself from degrading associations, and becomes ennobled and purified. This character, made by himself, transforms him. He has made, for the time, a divinity; and this divinity becomes his leader, strengthener, purifier, and inspirer. The God within us seeks for incarnation no less than the God without us; and the philosophical basis of the influence upon men of the incarnation of God's ideal is identical with that of the influence of their own incarnated ideals.

From this illustration I proceed to the proposition that it does not matter what legitimate passion or sentiment may be called out with relation to an object, the result will always be the same in kind, if not in degree. We may admire, revere, esteem, love, and in many ways enjoy, through the exhibition to us of an infinite variety of characteristics; and our admiration, reverence, esteem, love, and enjoyment, become the basis of the structure of ideals which shape the model of our own character, and inspire the life which it evolves. Idolatry is but the enthronement of the ideals of men who are ignorant of the true God. These ideals are formed of the highest qualities and conceptions of those who make them. They may be very low, but they shape the life of the people that produce them. Mari olatry is the worship of a very pure ideal, and the tributes offered to the multiplied saints of the Roman calendar are all paid to the incarnations of the noblest conceptions of their devotees. The marvellous gift of song possessed by Jenny Lind makes her very admirable to us; so we clothe her with the loveliest attributes, and make her a goddess. The real power of Washington upon the American mind is exerted, not by his simple self, but by his character, modified, magnified, exalted, harmonized, and enthroned by that mind, as the impersonation of its highest conception of patriotism. In the American imagination, he is a demi-god—a grand Colossus—before whose august shade we stand as pigmies. "All history is a lie," simply because no man can write it without being attracted to characters in such a way as to make ideals of them, and thus to throw all the facts connected with them out of their legitimate relations.

I repeat the statement, that ideals are the world's masters. They order our life, they dictate the form of our history, they are the very essence of poetry, and the staple of all worthy fiction. Our affections choose an object, and straightway our imaginations lift it into apotheosis. We garner in it that which is best in our thought, and it becomes a power upon us for the elevation of our life.

I have attempted thus far only to reveal and illustrate one of the most beautiful laws of mental action and re-action with which I am acquainted; and if my reader is as much interested in it as I am, he will follow me into a consideration of its bearings upon Christianity. I do not moot the question of the nature of the founder of Christianity,—that is, I do not say that Christ was God, or was not God,—but I say, what few will dispute, that he was God's incarnated ideal of a man—that Christ was all of God and his attributes that could be put into a man. It follows, that unless we can fully comprehend God's ideal, the Christ that we hold is our own ideal; and his power upon us is measured and described by the character of our ideal. "What think ye of Christ?" The answer to this great question, addressed to a soul or a sect, defines the type of Christianity possessed by such a soul or sect. He is what He is, a complete and definite character, but what we think of Him—our ideal of Him—determines the exact measure and kind of power with which He inspires us, and the quality and extent of the development He works in us.

It does not matter to this discussion whether Christ be what we believe Him to be, or a myth. If we admit that He is the first fact in the Christian system of religion, and the primary source of all inspiration to Christian movement and progress, it will follow that every soul and every sect must possess the highest possible idea of Christ before it can reach its highest point of development and its highest style of Christian life. According to our ideal of Christ—in the measure by which we invest Him with great attributes and authority—does He become to us an inspiring force. A person who thinks that Christ was only a good man, with frailties like other men,—an individual who lived a very pure life—a reformer—can possess only a very shallow Christian piety, because he can find in his ideal of Christ no inspiration to a piety more profound. A man who thinks the grand characteristics of Christ were meekness, self-denial, and patience under injury, without apprehending the other side of His character, will be a mean and abject man. A man who thinks that there was nothing in Christ but love—that contempt of all meanness, supreme reverence for justice, displeasure with all sin, and hatred of all cruelty and oppression, had no place in Him, will expend his sympathy on prisoners, and build palaces for convicts; and circulate petitions for the abrogation of death penalties.

If the doctrine I have advanced be sound, it is not necessary to refer to history to prove that the progress of Christianity has depended in all the past, (nor is the gift of prophecy requisite to the assertion that it will depend in all the future,) upon the prevalent ideal of Christ. The stream cannot rise higher than its fountain. Christ, as the inspirer of Christian life, is to the Christian world what that world makes Him to be. He must keep forever in advance of us, or there is no such thing as an infinite Christian progression. If there shall ever arrive a point in the history of any soul when its conception of Christ will cease to be higher than its own life, then that soul will have exhausted Christianity, and must stand still. If the history and being of Christ, as delineated by the Evangelists, forbid the world to form of Him the highest ideal which it is possible for it to conceive (which, of course, I do not believe), then those delineations must ultimately, by a philosophical necessity, become an insurmountable obstacle to the development of the highest style of Christianity of which the world is capable. I believe there is no proposition in moral philosophy more clearly demonstrable than this, and I hold myself in no way responsible for the conclusions to which it leads.

I believe in the proverb that any religion is better

than no religion, because every man's conception of goodness and duty is an advance of his character; and when this conception is imbodied in an object of worship, it becomes an elevating power upon his life that makes him capable of a certain degree of civilization. All the ideals of all ages have been developed in the direction of the perfect man—toward God's ideal. The shadowy gods that were grouped about Olympus were voiceless echoes of poor hearts crying after this perfect man. Hugh Miller, the inspired apostle of Science, found the rudiments of Christ in the rocks, and may we not find them in the souls of men? He found Jesus Christ in every lamina of the earth's crust; and as, with faith in his heart and the iron in his hand, he toiled among the old red sandstone, he saw the fossil flora of his own Scotch hills tipped with tongues of flame and the fauna rigid with the stress of prophecy. It was as if the blood of Calvary had stained and informed with meaning the insensate mass in which he wrought; or as if he were, with a divine instinct, hewing away the rock from the door of the sepulchre where the ages had laid his Lord. With a vision that was too wonderful and too glorious for the protracted entertainment of his mighty brain, he saw the varied forms of life climbing through the rugged centuries, and leaping from creation to creation, until they took resolution in the union of matter and spirit in man.

But science with a pining heart behind it was not satisfied even then. Not until the complex creature man was united with God was the chain complete. Then, with the last link fastened to The Throne, the grand riddle of "the Lamb slain from the foundation of the world" swung clear in the sight of angels and of men. So, to the delver in the stratified history of the race, do the dead ideals point toward and prophesy the advent and the character of the divine man.

Any religion is better than no religion because there exists in the ideal which inspires it a rudiment of Christ, and there is nothing in any religion that tends in any direct and legitimate way to the good of the soul which entertains it that is not a fraction or fragment of Christianity. Now it is manifest that every soul which gives in its allegiance to a fragmentary ideal of Christ stands really, for the time, upon the plane of paganism. In the degree in which Plato's ideal man, or ideal god, was greater than any given Christian's ideal Christ, was his paganism better than that Christian's Christianity—better in its essence, and better in its practical power upon life. The moment that a mind definitely circumscribes, measures, weighs, and comprehends its Christ, it limits its own Christian development, by fixing a point beyond which no Christian inspiration will come to it. The moment we cease to grow "in the knowledge of Jesus Christ," because there is no more to know of him, God's ideal will become inferior to our ideal, for reaching it we shall immediately conceive an ideal beyond it, in accordance with that law of progress which always keeps our conceptions of goodness and greatness in advance of our life. So I ask the question: will God's Christ answer the purpose of eternal progress, or will the time come when we shall be obliged to make a Christ for ourselves? I let every man answer this question in his own way.

This leads me to a thought which I consider of the highest practical importance to the Christian world, and which I should be glad to develop more fully than my space will allow. If the view which I have presented of the law of progress in Christian life be correct, then theology is a progressive science, and there is, and there can be, no standard of belief and faith good for all ages. As our ideal of Christ grows toward, or into, God's ideal, will that ideal change its relation to all the great facts of theology, as they are now comprehended by theologians. The theological systems of men and schools of men are determined always by the character of their ideal of Christ, the central fact of the Christian system. All the other facts arrange themselves around this ideal, and in harmony with it. Thus, as our ideal advances, gathering new glory and greatness and goodness, will certain doctrines which we now consider essential recede into insignificance, and others now scarcely insisted upon spring into prominence, and others still, now unknown, will be developed. Preachers and professors, churches and synods, may protest against innovations, but they must come by necessity, if there be any genuine Christian progress. A prescriptive standard of faith in Christianity—a system of everlasting progress—must forever remain an officious and sacrilegious intermeddling with the grand fundamental law of Christianity.

There is a time coming when all the sects which now divide Christendom will be melted into one. Nothing but the blotting out of Christianity can hinder it. My Presbyterian friend has his fragmentary ideal of Christ, my Episcopal friend another, my Roman Catholic friend another, and so on, through Baptists, Methodists, Universalists, and all the rest; but as the Christian world's ideal of Christ advances, and he is apprehended in something of the fulness of his being and character, will the world's theologies approach each other. They must do so, and they are doing so to-day. The best evidence in the world that Christianity is advancing is found in the fact that the walls between the sects are growing weaker, or falling in ruins. When they all come up to the point of any thing like a just idea of the sun in the centre of their systems, they will find that there is no difference between them. Therefore, let our ideal be kept well in advance, and always in advance; and let that ideal be the law of a man's theology. If my neighbor's ideal of Christ be better than mine, then, not only his life, but his system of theology, will be better than mine; and God forbid that I should curb him, or try to impose upon him my ideal and my theology. Ah, these Procrustean prescripts of belief—what unspeakably useless things are they!

VII.

PROVIDENCE.

"Man proposes and God disposes."
"Saint cannot, if God will not."
"Nothing is lost on a journey by stopping to pray or to feed your horse."
"God puts a good root in the little pig's way."
"God gives every bird its food, but does not throw it into the nest."
"He that is at sea has not the wind in his hands."

THE progress of modern science, the opulence of modern invention, and the splendor of modern achievement in the arts, are themes of ceaseless glorying and gratulation. I rejoice with the gladdest, and glory with the proudest; yet I feel that the world around me and the world within me have lost something, even more precious than they have gained—not irrecoverably, but, for the time, practically. The more the knowledge of material things has crowded in upon the apprehension of the world—the more the world has learned of the laws of matter, and the more stupendous the results it has achieved by laying those laws under tribute—the more from a large class of minds has faith retired, and Providence become a meaningless name. We drive toward materialism. We have become practical believers in necessity. Every thing is controlled by law. The machine has been wound up, the being who made and set it in operation has retired, and all that we can do is to fall into our place, and be borne on, careful only that no cog-wheel catch our fingers, and no weight descend upon our heads.

It is not only the irreligious world that disbelieves in Providence. I am inclined to think that there are Christians in large numbers who never dream of receiving blessings in answer to their prayers—Christians who would be absolutely startled with the thought that God had directly, and with special purpose, granted one of their petitions. God has come to be "counted out of the ring." Practically, we believe that He never interferes with the operation of one of His own laws—that no influence, under the control of His will, acting from daily and momently arising motives, can, or does, act with supreme power upon the chain of cause and effect established at the creation of the universe. Too much, even in the Christian imagination, God is a prisoner, shut up within the walls of His own laws—a Being who has farmed out the universe to the great firm of Laws and Principles, and is quietly waiting, with nothing to do, and no power to do any thing, till the lease expire. The man who declared that there was no use in praying for rain so long as the wind was in the north, illustrates the essential position of every nine minds in ten throughout Christendom. This, I know, is a sweeping statement, and I shall be very glad to be convicted of its falsehood. There is, doubtless, a strife constantly going on in a great multitude of minds to escape from the clutch of laws, and to find a Father's embrace, yet the majority of them "take things as they come," and, at most, expect God to do only those things for them which are outside the strict domain of natural law. Law is God, practically—Law, a thing of God, an institution born of Him, is put in His place, and He is shut out behind it. Thus the world is turned into a great mill, established on certain principles for the grinding out of certain results; and into the hopper all this great aggregate of individuals is poured like grain to be ground.

I will not say that the absorption of the modern mind in scientific studies and the production of great material results is entirely responsible for this reduction of the universe to essential orphanage, but its tendency, joined to the natural gravitation of our appetites and passions, has had the decisive power to sink us in that direction. To reveal this tendency to those in whom it unconsciously exists, and to counteract it so far as I have any power, is the present aim.

God is either supreme or subject. If subject, then I become an Atheist at once, for a subject God is no God. If He has passed over the line of my life to the control of a law, or a series of laws, then, so far as I am concerned, He is dethroned. If any law of the universe stands between me and the direct ministry of God to my wants and my worthy wishes and aspirations, then I may as well pray to my next door neighbor as to Him. Thus Providence is to me a question which involves the existence of a God. If law is a greater and a more powerful thing than He who established it, then, to me, He is practically of no account. I live and move and have my being in law, and not in Him. I sprang from law, I exist in law, and I am carried on by law I know not whither. If God pity me, He cannot help me. If He would save me, He cannot. Between Him and me His law places an impassable gulf, across which we may stretch our helpless hands toward each other to all eternity without avail. He is a prisoner, and I am a prisoner; and I may legitimately pity His weakness as much as he pities mine.

Again, God is either benevolent in His feelings toward each individual child in His universe, or He is utterly indifferent, or positively malicious. We look to Him as the author of all things—as the father of our spirits and the maker of our bodies, no more than as the author and founder of all law. If I decide in my mind that He has voluntarily placed it out of His power to help me, by instituting between me and Him a law which shuts Him from direct ministry to me, I decide, in effect, that He is indifferent to me, or malicious toward me. When I decide this, I dethrone Him just as essentially as when I decide that He is subject to His own law, and helpless in regard to its operation; for a God who is either indifferent or malicious has no claim upon my fealty or my affection. A God who does not love me has no claim upon my love. A God who voluntarily puts it beyond His power to aid me, or do me good, puts it equally beyond His power to do me direct harm. He is, therefore, nothing to me.

Thus, if there be not a God of Providence who ministers to my daily individual wants, and prescribes for me the discipline of my life—a God who hears me when I cry to Him, and holds immediate relations with every moment of my life, so far as I am concerned, there is no God at all. Ah! but there is a God. Few are the men who doubt this, and they are not those who would be convinced of their error by argument of mine. All healthy souls recognize the existence of this Being, and recognize among His attributes utter supremacy and infinite benevolence. Now the point that I make is this: that the moment we recognize God as supreme in power and infinitely good and loving toward all His intelligent creatures, that moment we admit the doctrine of universal and special Providence. There is no God, and there can be none, who is not a God of Providence. It is only to such a God that we can pray. It is only such a God that can, by possibility, call out our affections, or hold us to allegiance. Every thing that passes under the name of religion becomes a mockery and a delusion the moment we place Him behind laws which, like prison-bars, restrain Him from all participation in human affairs.

I know too well that in this thing I am not setting up and endeavoring to bring down a man of straw. I know many men who are professedly, at least, men of prayer, yet who declare in terms that the benefits of prayer are only to be looked for in the exercise of prayer. They attempt to explain the matter philosophically. There is something in the humble attitude of the soul before its Maker, incident to prayer—something in confession and the exercise of penitence—something in abstraction from worldly and impure thoughts—which, really, has the power to do great good, and in which reside all the benefits of prayer. While I recognize the immediate benefits of prayer as a mental and moral exercise, this partial and unworthy view of it is to me utterly contemptible. A man on his knees talking to God as if He could help him, yet believing that He will not, or cannot, and praying for blessings which he has no reason to expect, is a sight to be pitied of angels and of men. If this be all of prayer, it is an insult to a man, either to ask or command him to pray. Low as human dignity is, it would be compromised, and, if in any degree sensitive, offended, by being forced into attitudes and language which are a sham and a lie, for the purpose of securing incidental results of good.

No, prayer is not a legitimate, it is not even a decent and dignified, exercise, unless offered to a God of Providence who knows and is interested in all our affairs, is able to interfere with them and change their order through or above law, and is willing to do so, according as the motives in which our petitions are based show us ready for the reception of the blessings which we seek, and He in infinite paternal benevolence is ready to bestow. Well, we are commanded to pray throughout the Bible. We are promised answers to prayer, in no ambiguous language, throughout the Bible. We are taught after what manner to pray, by Him who spake as never man spake—Humanity's Great Teacher; and to the truly faithful Christian heart this should forever settle the question of Providence.

There is to me no thought more precious than that my Maker is my constant minister, direct and immediate. There is no thought that would sooner drive me mad than that I am in the iron grasp of laws which will work out their results within me and around me though they tear me in pieces, while the Maker of those laws and of me cannot help me, though I cry to Him out of the depths of my helplessness and distress. A natural law is only one of the regular rules by which, for good purposes, God works. It exists as a rule only by His constant will; and, in my opinion, drawn from every available analogy, He has a myriad irregular ways of reaching an end to one which is regular—ways constantly starting out from new impulses born of new motives within Him. The regular way of reaching New York or Washington is by a certain railroad, but I can reach either city by countless irregular ways, as circumstances or motives may dictate and direct. I may reach either city by other railroads less direct, yet having the same termination, as my will may decide; and to confine the supreme will of the universe to such regular channels of action as we happen to be acquainted with, is to assume that that will is weaker than our own.

I assume, that without a belief in a general and special Providence, no man who thinks at all upon the subject can be truly happy. We are all breakers of law—we are a race of law-breakers. The moment the mind swings loose from a belief in Providence, it plunges helpless and overwhelmed into a wild waste of penalties, from which there is and can be no extrication while existence endures. What has the history of the race been but that of law-breaking? Yet in spite of this—in spite of a violation which has become the habit of the world—it lives, and, thank God! progresses toward goodness. If law had been left alone of God's Providence to work out its own blind ends, there would not be a breathing man upon the face of the earth to-day. It is for the reason that we live and move and have our being in God, and not in law, that there rises to Heaven the smoke of a single city, or waves upon the hillside the burden of a single cultivated harvest.

Let no man be deceived by that subtlest of all infidelities which dethrones a God of Providence. The very hairs of our heads are numbered by Him, and not even he life of a sparrow that He has made is extinguished without His notice. There is not an infant's wail, a sigh of anguish, a groan of pain, or a word of prayer, breathed in the humblest abode, that He does not hear. Over all our struggles and toils He stoops with a loving eye, and with a heart anxious that the discipline He has established for us may do us good. He knows all our doubts and fears; He rejoices in all our worthy hopes and joys. When we kneel He sees us; when we pray He hears. His presence envelopes us, His knowledge comprehends us, His power upholds us. All law and all being are alike dependent, moment by moment, upon Him for existence. The ultimate root of every flower that bends beneath its weight of dew is planted in His will. It is His breath that breaks the bosom of the sea into billows; it is His smile that soothes it into rest. The blue sky that bends over us is but the visible image of His loving bosom, holding myriad worlds in the infinite depths of its tenderness. Ah, let it never be hidden to the eye of faith by the showers of blessings which come from it, borne on the wings of natural law!

I know of no skepticism more fatal to the development of religion in the heart than that which dethrones a God of Providence. In vain shall we look for a true piety among those who, through absorption in scientific pursuits, or devotion to the details of natural law in mechanical and similar callings, are brought to the deification of law. Law has no love, no pity, no mercy, no patience. Law has nothing in it to touch our sympathies, or call out our affections. If it have power in an indirect way to rouse within us a sense of esponsibility for our conduct, it is only to curse us with the thought that it has no power to forgive. The idea that man can be truly religious, with a God voluntarily bereft of power for good or evil, is simply absurd. We never find, and we never can find, true piety in a heart that does not so thoroughly believe in a God of Providence that it can pray with an honest faith that God can grant its petition.

It is well that we have law, that we understand it, and that we obey it. Law is essential to our highest liberty. It defines the bounds within which we may safely be allowed to exercise our wills, and work out our destiny. It draws the lines along which we may legitimately labor in the development of our powers. It reveals the relations which exist between material things and ourselves. Law is never to be ignored as an important part of the machinery by which its founder administers the world's great affairs, but we are never to shut God out of it, nor to shut him behind it. It is intended that we shall accomplish all through law that we can accomplish for ourselves—that we shall earn by the use of law all that we can earn for physical sustenance, and our spiritual satisfaction. God gives every bird its food, but does not throw it into the nest. He does not unearth the good which the earth contains, but He puts it in our way, and gives us the means of getting it ourselves.

The time has already come to multitudes of men when the providence which orders their lives is a demonstrated reality. There is no tractable soul that has, by yielding to the indications of the supreme will, and obeying law, worked its way into the light, that does not recognize a wisdom and purpose in its life and history superior to, and independent of, itself, and the laws within and around it. In darkness or light this demonstration will ultimately come to all. It shall be seen by every soul that the discipline of its life was chosen in infinite wisdom as that which was best calculated to enlarge and ennoble it, whether it produce the desired result or not. To all souls emancipated from the clutches of necessity, and clinging with love and faith to the hand of the Great Dispenser, life becomes a great and glorious thing. They recognize every affliction, every reverse, every pain, as portions or features of an infinitely beneficent ministry. Every joy that visits them, every hope that cheers them, every good that they receive, is a renewed testimony of the love in which they are held by Him who has ordered their life in the past, and who is pledged by all His previous ministry to lead it to its divinest issues. It is to this height of human happiness that I would lead the blind, mistaken, discontented spirits that grope among laws as blind as themselves. Poor orphans! Happy for you is it that your belief, or lack of belief, does not shut out Providence from you, nor hinder its constant efforts to bring you to its recognition!

VIII.

DOES SENSUALITY PAY?

"Cent. per cent. do we pay for every vicious indulgence."

"If you pursue good with labor, the labor passes away, but the good remains; if you pursue evil with pleasure, the pleasure passes away but the evil remains."

"Virtue and happiness are mother and daughter."

LIFE would appear to be a very dangerous sea, judging by the number of wrecks that strew its shores—more remarkably unsafe, perhaps, for pleasure yachts and such other fancy craft as may fail to maintain the proper relations between canvas and ballast. I know of no object of contemplation more sad than a human wreck. I can look upon death when it brings release to a happy soul, or even to a miserable body, with an emotion akin to satisfaction; I can contemplate a great calamity, when it involves no stain of honor and no loss of character, with equanimity—content that the hand of Providence is in it, and that good must consequently come out of it; I can read cf great conflicts upon the battle-field, where the atmosphere is burdened by expiring life, and blood flows in rivers, and rise from the picture inspired by its heroisms; but I cannot look upon a human wreck, a lost life, a ruined man or woman, without being sick with horror, or saddened into an unspeakable pity. To think of youth's bright hopes and precious innocence—of love of truth and purity—of honor, and manhood, and womanhood—of genius and talent—of all goodly gifts of person and graces of mind—of all sweet affections and aspirations gone down—down into the abyss of perdition, blotted out or spoiled—ah, this is, by awful eminence, the horror of the world!

Yet visions of ruined men and women are not uncommon. We walk out into the world on some pleasant day, every thing fair and fresh around us, and, with health in our blood and peace in our hearts, we think how good and beautiful a thing life is; yet we rarely walk far without meeting some one to whom all its goodness and beauty are lost. We meet some wretch whose haggard face and feeble limbs and fetid breath betray the victim of debauchery, dying by his last foul disease. Behind him walks the bloated form of one who has surrendered his will to his appetite. His bloodshot, meaningless eyes, and heavy, staggering feet, give index to the curse which is upon him. We turn our eyes away from him with a shudder, but only to be greeted by a sight that makes us still more sad. We meet a form of beauty—a woman—but the wanton grace of her step, the artificial flush upon her cheek, the hollow eye and brazen gaze, tell of the prostitution or loss of that which seems to us the one angelic element of the world. All these are human wrecks—lost lives—men and women who have surrendered all that is best in them to that which is basest—men and women who have turned their backs upon God and heaven, and gone down into a very hell of beastliness. Whence and why are these wrecks? Let us see.

In the constitution of man—a constitution which associates spirit with matter by marvellous marriage of organisms, and intimately interchanging sympathies, and subtle interdependences—the Creator has so constructed the body that it shall convey to the mind, for its comprehension, the properties and qualities of material things. These properties and qualities are communicated by and through the senses, and these senses are so constituted as, in their exercise and office, to affect us by pleasure or by pain. Chiefly the office of the senses is that of conveying pleasure. For the sense of smell, the vital alchemy at work in the flowers elaborates an infinite variety of perfumes. For the sense of taste, the food is prepared in meats and fruits and grains of an infinite variety of flavors. The auditory sense is regaled by birds and brooks, by instruments which the cunning hand of man has made, and by that greatest of all instruments, the human voice. Light ministers to the pleasure of vision, reflected by numberless forms of beauty. In fact, there is no pathway that leads into the penetralia of our natures, and gives passage to the comprehension of the good things of God, that does not absorb something of the divine aroma of that which it bears. The process of eating, by which we prepare for deglutition the food necessary for our support, is a process of pleasure. We do not gorge our food like the anaconda, impelled by a bald and beastly greed; but its qualities please our senses.

Now, so long as these senses are kept to their appropriate ministry—always a subordinate one, in that they deal entirely with the qualities and properties of matter—so long will it be well with the soul to which they minister; but whenever the soul turns to them as the source of its highest pleasures, and seeks for the multiplication and intension of those pleasures as the great end of its life, then the whole being is prostituted, and absolute, unmixed evil is the natural and inevitable result. There is no law in the universe more certain in its operation than that which punishes sensuality. The man who makes a god of his belly feels the result in an unwieldy, gouty frame and a stupid brain. The man who delights in the intoxication of his senses by the use of stimulants, wears them out, and poisons, even to their death, both body and soul. The man and the woman who seek, by the gratification of desires unchastened by love and unwarranted by law, to filch from a heaven-ordained relation the delights of its hallowed commerce, and give themselves up to this form of sensuality, never fail to win to themselves moral corruption or induration, and bodily imbecility and disease. At the gate of this garden of sensual pleasure the angel stands with his sword of flame, and no man enters unsmitten of him. In the path of sensuality, in all its multiplied forms, God has placed barriers mountain-high, to stop men, and frighten them back from the certain degradation and destruction to which it leads. The path to life is in the opposite direction.

I have said thus much upon the philosophy of the prostitution of the soul to sense, that I might the more readily reach the convictions of a generation which, active as it is in intellectual and Christian development, has stronger tendencies to sensuality than any of its predecessors in this country. As wealth increases in any country, the tendencies to sensuality, through the temptations of idleness and the growth of the means of gratification, always increase. The history of national decline and downfall is but a detail of the effects of sensuality. The elevation of style in living beyond a certain point, always impinges on the sensual. Beyond this point, that which we call luxury commences, and luxury is but sensuality refined. In this country we are all seeking for luxury ; and those who cannot afford it, associated with homes, home pleasures, and home restraints, embrace such forms of sensual gratification as come within their means to purchase. Men who are poor, look on with envy, and are seeking on every side, in new philosophies and systems, and phases of religion, for the license which shall give them more of sense with smaller drafts on conscience. As the free spirit of the age breaks away from bondage to old ideas, old bigotries, and old superstitions, it goes wild, and in its newly-found liberty runs daringly and blindly into forbidden fields. The free-love doctrines and free-love practices of the day, the multiplication of cases of divorce, and the shameful infidelities that prevail, are all indications of the sensual tendencies of the age.

Where penalty succeeds so poorly, there may seem to be rather poor encouragement for preaching; but, in my opinion, the teachers and preachers of the age should direct more of their power against a tendency which is doing more to undermine the character of the American people than their sateless thirst for gold. Even in the general strife for wealth, the desire for luxury is largely the motive power. The object kept prominently in view is feasting—eye-feasting, ear-feasting, tongue-feasting, or the feasting of other or of all the senses—and this beyond natural desire, and with the wish and intent to coax from the organs cf sense more of pleasure than they can afford with health to themselves and the souls to which they minister.

Now, my opinion is, that to a man, or a body of men, prostituted or in process of prostitution to sense, there is very little use in talking of religion or morals. Those are motives which they do not understand. So I address myself to the selfishness of the age, as a motive, the strength of which may not be questioned, and bid it withdraw its hand from this fire on pain of losing it. "Cent. per cent. do we pay for every vicious indulgence," says the proverb; but it is too moderate by half in its estimate of expense, for a youth of sensual pleasure can never compensate for a life of pain. If you do not believe this, ask the debauchee whose senses and sensibilities were long since burned to ashes. Seek further testimony, if you will, of her whose brief life of sensuality is closed by abandonment; or of him whose gluttony has made him a disgustingly bulky bundle of ailments, or of him whose nerves shiver with the poison on which they live. If you say that I am deal ing with extremes, without analogies to yourselves, retire into your own consciousness, and question what you find there—old sins of sense that start up and fill you with remorse and fear—old wounds of conscience gaping and bleeding still—old fractures of character that refuse to unite, and make you shudder at your own weakness—old stains upon your purity that memory will not allow to fade. This process will prove to any man of ordinary weakness, who has been subjected to ordinary temptations, that never, in a single instance, has he indulged in an unlawful sensual pleasure without paying for it a thousand times in pain.

The universal fact, based in universal experience, is, that there is nothing in the world that makes so poor a return for its cost as sensual pleasure. No man ever traded extensively in this line without becoming a bankrupt in happiness. It does not pay, and cannot be made to pay, and every man would see and understand this if he would keep an account of his receipts and expenditures. Let me help you to open a book of this kind. Credit sensual pleasure for a spree—a night of hilarity, produced by drinking and feasting; and then turn to the other side of the account, and debit it with the details of cost—money enough to furnish bread for a hundred hungry mouths; a day of languor, pain, and indolence; a damaged reputation which may interfere with the projects and prospects of a whole life; a loss of self-respect, and a deadening of moral sensibility; a reduction of the capacity of enjoyment and of the stock of vitality; the sullen pangs of a reproving conscience; the tears of a mother and the severer anguish of a father,—all these, and more, for an hour of artificial insanity! How does the account look?

Suppose we try another: Credit Sensual Pleasure for the illicit indulgence of a powerful passion. Then place the cost upon the debit side of the ledger: shame and fear, conscious loss of purity, the possession of a foul secret that is to be carried into all society, and into all relationships, disease and remorse, or, what is more than all these, hardness, brutality, and the formation of habits whose only end is ruin. I may not, through fear of giving offence, enter into all the details of the debit side of this account. They may be found and read of all men in graveyards, in hospitals, in brothels, in gar rets, and cellars, in ruined families, and ruined hearts and hopes. Now does this thing pay?

I have presented only the private side of this ac count, and that but imperfectly. There is a public side. The innumerable paupers, whose life is supported by the State, owe their pauperism, directly or remotely, in three cases out of four, to sensuality—to strong drink, licentiousness, or some form of extravagance that proceeded from a devotion to sensual pleasure. Idiots begotten in drunkenness, lunatics through various forms of sensual vice, criminals whc are caged in every jail and prison like wild beasts, diseased creatures, alike loathsome to themselves and others, crowded into numberless pestilent hospitals,—all these are public burdens.

imposed by the sins of sensuality. If we run through the whole catalogue of crimes, we shall find them all growing directly or indirectly out of this comprehensive vice. In fact, it may be said that all crime, with all its consequences, is but a manifestation of the dominance of sense over reason and conscience.

In this view—and no one knows better than its victims that it is the correct view—Sensuality rises into the position of the grand scourge of mankind. It is the mother of disease, the nurse of crime, the burden of taxation, and the destroyer of souls. Oh, if the world could rise out of this swamp of sensuality, rank with weeds and dank with deadly vapors—full of vipers, thick with pitfalls, and lurid with deceptive lights, and stand upon the secure heights of virtue where God's sun shines, and the winds of heaven breathe blandly and healthfully, how would human life become blessed and beautiful! The great burden of the world rolled off, how would it spring forward into a grand career of prosperity and progress! This change, for this country, rests almost entirely with the young men of the country. It lies with them more than any other class, and more than all other classes, to say whether this country shall descend still lower in its path to brutality, or rise higher than the standard of its loftiest dreams. The devotees of sense, themselves, have greatly lost their power for good, and comparatively few will change their course of life. Woman will be pure if man will be true. Young men, this great result abides with you. If you could but see how beautiful a flower grows upon the thorny stalk of self-denial, you would give the plant the honor it deserves. If it seem hard and homely, despise it not, for in it sleeps the beauty of heaven and the breath of angels. If you do not witness the glory of its blossoming during the day of life, its petals will open when the night of death comes, and gladden your closing eyes with their marvellous loveliness, and fill your soul with their grateful perfume.

IX.

THE WAY TO GROW OLD.

"Good morrow, glasses! Farewell lasses!"
"All wish to live long, but none to be called old."
"Every dog has his day."
"A hundred years hence we shall all be bald."
"If you would not live to be old, you must be hanged when you are young."

IF we except the Chinese, (who have a remarkable talent for being exceptions to general rules,) all men and women make an idol of youth. Manhood in its fresh embodiment—healthful, strong, and majestic—and womanhood in its rosy morning—fragrant with sweet thoughts and hopes, and radiant in its dewy beauty—attract the love and admiration of all—perhaps even the envy of many. Childhood looks up to them, and longs to grow to their estate. Old age regards the memory of them with a sigh, and rarely fails to find in them its most congenial society. We walk to our mirrors, and scan with gathering sadness the lines that the graver of care has traced, and pluck from our temples, with unhappy surprise, the first stark threads of silver that Time slips through our chance-thrown locks, or inlays upon their plaited black and brown; yet "we feel as young as we ever did." We are not estranged from the young, but stand among them with strong hands and hearts, unable to realize that they look upon us as men and women who are "getting considerably along in the world." The cheek and lip of Beauty, her sparkling eyes, and plump outline, and graceful and elastic step, touch us with the same thrill of pleasure that they did in the early days of sympathy and passion. Youth—ah! Beautiful Gate of the Temple of Life! It matters little how gorgeous the temple may be when entered,—how majestic the arches, how long the vista, how richly illuminated and emblazoned the windows, or how heavenly the music that thrills its iris-tinted silences,—we never forget the precious moments spent in lingering at the portal, the glorious rosette above it, and the sky-born melody of the chimes that filled our ears and hearts with welcome.

Our life's ideal is always filled with the blood and breath of youth. Our finest conceptions of human beauty evermore embrace youth as their prime element. Strength, enthusiasm, hope, purity, love,—all these when combined and embodied in their most attractive forms, rise in our imaginations as youthful attributes. So true is this, that in looking forward to the day when the dust of those who have gone before us into the land of spirits shall rise, and assume the forms they are to wear in the celestial city, there springs up always a vision of their youth. We expect to meet the tottering father whose eyes we closed, and whose wasted and feeble limbs we composed, as young, and fresh, and strong as when he bore us to the baptismal font. There are to be no thin, silvery curls upon the brow of the mother, but in some sweet way, all the hallowed graces of maternity and the unfathomable tenderness of a soul disciplined by sorrow are to be associated—interfused—with the beauty and the youth of the bride. Immortality—twin-sister of Eternity—is always young, and brings no thought of age and decay. An angel with a wrinkle? A cherub with a feeble or a weary wing? We cannot imagine such beings. Heaven and everlasting youth are inseparable thoughts.

So it is that the first consciousness we have of growing old comes to us with a pang. There seems to be something unnatural in it. We feel the soul within us expanding, and know that its vision is clearer, its power greater, and its capacity for happiness diviner, yet the body in which this soul lives shows signs of decay. There is an increasing incompatibility between the tenant and the tenement. Some people feel so badly about it that they undertake to repair the old tabernacle—to put in porcelain teeth, and dye their hair, and don artificial curls, and put on feathers and finery. It is all a pretty little device, and harmless, because it cheats nobody, and really makes the world better looking. And this brings me to what I desire to say touching the duty of growing old gracefully and happily.

There is a homely kind of philosophy that will help those who are not up to any thing higher. The alternative of growing old is dying young. The only way to keep hair from becoming gray is to have it clipped off as a memento of a departed man, or laid away to decay with him. Wrinkles are either to be made out in God's sunlight, among living things, by the hand of Time, or by worms working in the dark. I take it that there is an easy choice between these two evils, and that whatever the evidences may be that God has answered our wishes—whether gray hairs, or feeble knees, or dull sight—we should regard them with gratitude.

Again, keeping alive our sympathy with the race to which we belong, and manfully willing to take our chance with the rest, we should remember that when we perceive the signs of age upon ourselves, we have enjoyed our own single term of youth, like all men who have gone before us, and that those who come after us will have no more. Every dog has his day. Those who are young to-day, and who are doubtless the subjects of envy to some of us, will be old to-morrow. They are enjoying the day we have already enjoyed, and will soon reach the point where we are standing. It is an even thing; and it compromises all that is unselfish and chivalrous within us to wish for a better lot in this respect than is meted out to the rest of the great brotherhood of men. Still again, if we find the evidences of age creeping upon us, we cannot avoid their further encroachment except by committing suicide; and this would be a very bad alternative. What we cannot help, we must bear; and it is for our interest to bear it cheerfully. It is very pleasant to be young, but as the body can only be young once, the next best thing is to have the privilege of growing old. We are to remember that if we look back with regret to the period we have passed, the young are looking forward with hope that they may reach the period at which we have arrived. They may not like to be called old, but they all wish to live long.

But there is a better point than this from which to regard this matter. To go back to our theory that every thing immortal in its nature is, by necessity of that nature, young, I make the proposition that the secret of growing old gracefully and happily resides in the comprehension of this fact, and in the institution of such measures as may be necessary to keep a decay. ing body from infecting or injuring in any way the soul's health while attached to it. No man on God's footstool feels old, or realizes that he is old, whose soul has not been improperly affected by his body. The feeling of age in the mind is like the effect upon life of being in an old, damp house, dingy with dirt and reeking with rottenness,—more perhaps like the effect of the close, bed-fellow association of age and infancy—the former drawing off the vital forces of the latter, and imparting to it the taint of its diseases. There is no such thing as an old soul in the universe, but there are a great many diseased or depressed souls—diseased or depressed by a great variety of causes, prominent among which is the decay of the bodies which they inhabit.

The natural idolatry exercised by the old for the young, though owing greatly to the unpleasant associations of age, has a deeper meaning in it than we have generally comprehended. God turns our hearts toward the young that the influence of youth upon them may be a power conservative of their health, and preventive of the depressing influence of bodily age. It is a part of the beautiful ministry of children.to preserve uninjured by the passage of time the souls of those with whom they are associated; and in the general rule of life the Good Father provides children for those who live to middle age, and when those are grown up, He gives them grand-children, so that they shall never be without this beneficent influence. Those who remain unmarried, or are not blest with children, grow old in feeling as they grow old in years, from the lack of this influence upon them, though there are exceptions to this rule—the exceptions illustrating the principle even better or more forcibly than the general rule itself. There are some among the childless old who are passionately fond of children, and I have never known such men and women who were not genial, sunny, and young in feeling. They seem instinctively to turn to children for that influence, whatever it may be, which will preserve their souls from the depressing power of age. I make the broad proposition that there is not an old man or woman living, at this moment in close sympathy with the hearts and minds of children and youth, who feels the influence upon his or her soul of a decaying body.

The springs of the soul's life abide in the affections. If these are properly fed, either by love of the young, or by love in its higher and stronger manifestations, they mount into perennial youth. Next above the love of the young—special or universal—comes connubial love, as a conservator of the youthful feeling of the soul. Two married hearts that came together in early life, and have lived in the harmony and love which constitute real marriage, never grow old. The love they bear to one another is an immortal thing. It is as fond and tender as it was when they pledged their faith to each other at the altar. Such a love as this can rise from no other than an immortal fountain. The fires of passion may die, desire may burn out like a candle, yet chastened and purified, this love—a product of essential youth—becomes the conservator of youth. The pine produces its resin, and the resin preserves the pine from decay, centuries after the life that produced it has passed away. The little spring that bursts up from where nature prepares her waters for the healing of the nations, deposits for itself a wall which shuts out all impurities, and keeps it always sparkling and young.

Above this love—better than this and every other love—is the love of the soul for the Father Soul—the sympathy of that which is immortal in it for Him from whom it came. The man who comprehends his relation to this Being, and whose heart goes out toward Him in true filial affection, knows that age is only a word, and that it has no more relation to his soul than it has to God himself. God is doubtless intimately associated with this material universe. It is blent with all His plans. It is the organ in multitudinous methods of His thought. In many ways it is the means by which He manifests His will, so that, in a certain sense, we may regard it as a body of which He is the resident and president soul. Yet this universe is to wax old like a garment. It is to fade like our own bodies; but no one supposes that the old age of the universe will touch the immortal youth of its Maker. The extinguishment of one of the lamps that He has hung out in space brings no shadow upon His brow. The wreck of a sidereal system works no weakness in His arm. Wrapped in the aura of His own ineffable love, He lives; and because He lives, we shall live also; because He is immortally young shall we also be immortally young; because no organized material system, however intimately associated with Him, can affect, by its decay and wreck, the fountain of His life, the decay of our bodies, if we are like Him, and live in the same atmosphere of love, will not affect us, either in fact or feeling.

A man who lives wrapped in this atmosphere of love—love of children, love of a bosom companion, love of men, love of God—imparts to his decaying body something of the youth of the spirit within. As the body may and does affect the spirit when no counteracting agencies prevent, so does the spirit act upon the body as a preservative power when in its normal condition and exercise. Many an old man's and woman's face have I seen luminous with the fires of youth, outshining from the soul. The clogs are lifted from the mortal when the soul comes into sympathy with this element of immortality. The love that gushes for all is the real elixir of life—the fountain of bodily longevity. It is the lack of this that always produces the feeling of age. Upon a soul not filled and exercised by love, the decaying body encroaches with its weakness and poison, till the belief of many in the immortality of the soul—a soul independent of matter—becomes uprooted.

Whenever men or women find themselves losing their sympathy with youthful hearts and pursuits, they may be sure that something is wrong with them; for it is not in the nature of the soul to grow old. It may grow in height, and depth, and breadth, and power, but the passage of years can bring it no decay. Consequently, all those who feel themselves dissonances in the song which the young life around them is singing, are allowing their bodies to do their souls damage. I believe that every healthy old saint in Christendom finds his heart going out more and more towards the young. As his evening sun descends, and heaven grows glorious while the shadows gather upon the earth, he loves more and more to gather around him that which is essentially heavenly—young men and maidens, and the bright forms and innocent faces of children. Prepared for heaven, it is only in such society and that which sympathizes with it, that he finds his heart at home. I believe that social life, in all its healthful manifestations, is that which combines all ages—which brings youth and middle age together with old age and childhood. Every age needs the influence of every other age to keep it healthful. There is no such thing as age with those who, in a few years at most, will be as the angels in heaven. As we shall be, and as we shall associate, there, so should we be, and so should we associate here; and let this truth never fail to be remembered: that unless the aged sympathize with the young, they will get no sympathy, save in the form of pity, from the young. God does not send young sympathies in that direction. He always holds us back with them, while our bodies go on to decay and death, and we forget, in immortal youth, that we were ever old.

X.

ALMSGIVING.

> "Give and spend,
> And God will send."
>
> "Charity and pride have different aims, yet both feed the poor."
>
> "What the Abbot of Bamba cannot eat, he gives away for the good of his soul."
>
> "He steals a pig, and gives away the trotters for God's sake."

I HAVE no idea of absolute property but that which is born of absolute creation by an independent, self-existent power. There is but one genuine proprietor in the universe, and that proprietor is its Maker. All that we call ours—all that we win by toil, and are allowed to hold, for our use and at our disposal, by the laws of civil society—was made and is owned by Him who made and owns us. The mite that makes a home for itself in our cheese does not, by the processes of burrowing and feeding, institute a claim to property in the cheese. The robin that builds a nest in our maple, from materials selected upon our land, cannot be said to own the tree, if we have a purpose for it that interferes with her nest. That God is the grand proprietor must be received as a cardinal, vital fact by all who do not deny the existence of God himself. It is not for me to declare to the world the manner in which He regards this portion of His property; but I cannot help thinking that He looks upon it as a great mansion which He has taken infinite pains to construct for the shelter and support of a family of children in whom He takes infinite interest. These continents of verdure, this great and wide sea, swinging like a pendulum between its shores, overhung by the moon's mysterious dial, these rivers, nursed in their crystal infancy at the bosoms of these motherly hills and mountains, this downy atmosphere, that feeds our breath, and fans our brows, and springs over us its canopy of blue, this wonderful variety of animal life, that rejoices in forest wildernesses and smooth pastures, and swims in the sea and floats upon the air—all these were made and are supported by His power, for the benefit of the intelligent creatures whom He has placed among them.

Now, if we have any thing like ownership in these things, this ownership has its basis in God's beneficence. If we hold any thing by right, for our special use, and at our disposal, we hold it as a gift of God, and as a temporary gift. We are allowed to use these things for a time; and then we pass away, and they are transferred to the possession of others. Not unfrequently they are taken from us while we live. The patient Man of Uz exhibited his idea of property—the true idea—in the familiar words, "The Lord gave, and the Lord hath taken away." In making this world, the Creator furnished it with all the materials necessary for the support of His entire human family. For the best development of our minds and bodies, He made it necessary for us to labor, so that, by moulding the agencies and recombining the materials He permits us to use, we may secure that which is necessary for our sustenance and shelter. He knew that some would be able to secure more than enough for sustenance and shelter, and that others would not be able to secure enough, yet He did not intend that any should lack food and clothing, or any of the essentials of healthful bodily and mental life. He knew, and, I verily believe, intended, that some should be poor and that others should be rich; and thus instituted the emergency for human beneficence or charity. It is better, on the whole, that the world should be made up of benefactors and beneficiaries than that each man should be independent of every other man.

Thus, every man whom He has made, or whom He has allowed to become, rich, He has by that favor commissioned to be an almoner of His bounty to those whom He has not thus favored. The sick, the helpless, the utterly poor through misfortune—these are always with us. The Saviour Himself stated this as a fact good for all time; and I know of no man who dares to deny that these unfortunate ones have an absolute right to live, and, consequently, a right to so much of the property of others as may be necessary to support them. The pauper systems established by all Christian states have their basis in the absolute right of the helpless to aid at the hand of society. If you, who read these words, are rich, you recognize, every time you pay a tax for the comfort and support of those who can do nothing or little for themselves, the fact, that a portion of your wealth, at least, belongs to somebody else. Whether you recognize it or not, the fact is the same. What we call State charities, are essentially State equities. The lunatic asylums, the pauper establishments, the hospitals, the reform schools, all grow out of the duty which the element of wealth in society owes to the element of weakness.

But the State is a great body, and moves clumsily. There are countless fields of beneficent or charitable effort and privilege to which its operations are not fitted. There is a great amount of work which it neither can do, nor should do; and precisely here arise the duties of individual wealth to individual want—of individual wealth to the need of the world for food, raiment, Christian light, educational and religious institutions, and almost numberless schemes of public good. If, in the economy of Heaven, there exist the necessity of institutions and schemes for private and public good which are manifestly outside of the legitimate sphere of the State—institutions and schemes which can only be established by the contributions of wealth—it is as if God had laid His finger upon every rich man's purse, and pronounced the word, "Give!" What do you think God gave you more wealth than is requisite to satisfy your rational wants for, when you look around and see how many are in absolute need of that which you do not need? Can you not take the hint?

Men may give from a compassionate, or generous impulse—from a momentary excitement of their sympathies—and very much is given in this way, without doubt. I will not quarrel with this variety of charity; but I believe that a genuine spirit of beneficence can be exercised by no mind that does not recognize all the wealth it enjoys as the gift of God, to be shared with the children of penury, or devoted to institutions that contemplate the general good. God is the giver, life a partnership, humanity a brotherhood. The selfish accumulation, and sequestration from society of superfluous good, is at war with the economy of the Universe. Every thing in nature tends to equilibrium, and the universal compensation of expenditure. The rill takes the gift of the mountain spring and passes it on to the brook, and the brook pours the waters it receives into the river, and the river bears the burden of its gifts to the sea, and heaven itself descends to lift from the sea and return in cloud-winged argosies to the spring from whence they came the waters which it gave, and glorifies the spot by hanging over it the beauty of its rainbow. What earth sends up, heaven sends down, and what heaven sends down, earth returns. Circulation, diffusion, tendency by multiplied methods to equilibrium—these are the universal laws of nature. It is only man that hoards. It is only man that accumulates, and for selfish ends holds imprisoned superfluous good, and refuses to let it go out on its beneficent mission.

The charity of the day is, as a general thing, but a sorry apology for that beneficence which springs from a true apprehension of the primary source of wealth, its real ownership, and its legitimate uses. Millions have doubtless been given for the gratification of pride, and for the purpose of securing the applause of the world. If the time ever come when even and exact justice shall be meted out to the various agencies operative in the world toward beneficent results, the recipients of charity in its several forms will find themselves largely indebted to the devil. Bread is bread to the hungry, and clothing raiment to the naked, and the Bible light to the benighted. It does not matter to the needy from what source a charitable ministry proceed. If they are fed and clothed and enlightened, they have cause of satisfaction and gratitude, without questioning the sources of the good which reaches them.

I suppose that one of the severest trials of a sordid man is that which is caused by the disgust he feels in the society of his own soul. I once heard a preacher remark that were it not for the interposition of sleep, by which all men are separated once in twenty-four hours from the consciousness of their own meanness, they would all die of self-contempt. I judge the statement to be somewhat broad, but it holds within it a truth which lies at the basis of a moiety, more or less, of the charities of wealth. Every man who achieves riches by great speculations, by sharp practices, by trade which involves operations not altogether honorable, has his own method of maintaining self-complacency, or self-toleration; but his efforts usually take the form of charity. There is no scoundrel living who does not feel obliged to convince himself, in some way, that he is as good as the average of mankind. Poor scoundrels, who have no more than money enough to feed their vices and themselves, depreciate the excellence of the character about them, and win the self-complacency they seek by dragging it down to the dirt which defines their own level. Rich scoundrels, finding themselves respectable as the world goes, naturally resort to sacrifices—to throwing out and abandoning to the maw of the wolf that follows them some contemptible portion of gains gotten meanly and kept foully. Even the highway robber boasts that if he has taken from the rich, he has given to the poor. Not unfrequently these men, grown rich by doubtful courses, become special patrons of the church, or of educational institutions. We see them installed in the most expensive pews on Sunday, or adorning a select position devoted to the annual exhibition of a board of trustees.

But these are all comparatively tolerable men. They do good in the world, and evince a degree of sensitiveness which demands more or less of our sympathy. There is a form of self-conciliation, however, which would be laughable were its results less disastrous. Though not laughable, it is really admirable, as a specimen of the most perfect type of meanness; for I take it that every thing perfect in its kind is, in a sense, admirable. It is exhibited by those who undertake to satisfy themselves with themselves by initiating ecret schemes of good to go into operation after they are dead—schemes which, sooner than establish or assist, they would pluck their eyes out, if they were expecting to live forever. They are thus enabled to gratify their greed for gold—to overreach, exact usury, and hoard, and at the same time save themselves from a crushing self-contempt by contemplating in secret the fact that their gains are already devoted to a good end! But the devil never leaves them here. He induces them to trample under feet the sympathies and claims of consanguinity, to cut off with a dirty shilling old servants whose lives have been devoted to them, to institute schemes of beneficence impracticable even to ludicrousness, or to leave their wills so imperfectly drawn as to create quarrels among their natural heirs, and destroy the peace and harmony of families that will hold their memories fit subjects of execration so long as they hold them at all.

It is time that wealth in nominally Christian hands were bestowed upon the weak, the needy, and the suffering, from higher motives than a compassionate impulse or desire for public applause and private satisfaction. I know that it is very hard to admit that we do not hold our superfluous wealth and superabundant means by absolute right—that what we earn by toil or win by traffic is not ours to hoard or dispense at our pleasure; but if we are really and truly owners of what we possess, then beneficence is no duty. It is simply a favor shown to God through care for His unfortunate children, for which He owes us either adequate compensation or appropriate gratitude. The simple truth is, that in the degree by which a man's wealth is increased, is his family enlarged. Over against every pile of superfluous dollars, God places a pile of needs.

I account the office of benefactor, or almoner, to which God appoints all those whom he has favored with wealth, one of the most honorable and delightful in the world. He never institutes a channel for the passage of His bounties that those bounties do not enrich and beautify. The barren moor that parts before the steel of the mountain brook betrays the furrow by a fresher green and rarer flowers. Noble cities and all forms of beautiful life mirror themselves in rivers that become highways for the passage of commerce. God gives leaves to every stalk that bears juices up to the growing fruit, and presents a flower in advance to every twig that elaborates a seed. The sky weaves radiant garlands for itself from the clouds to which it gives transportation. So every man who becomes heartily and understandingly a channel of the divine beneficence, is enriched through every league of his life. Perennial satisfaction springs around and within him with perennial verdure. Flowers of gratitude and gladness bloom all along his pathway, and the melodious gurgle of the blessings he bears is echoed back by the melodious waves of the recipient stream.

We need at this period of the Christian development a more thorough recognition of the great truths I have endeavored to reveal. Churches are crippled with debt, or languish for efficient support. Educational institutions are begging for aid to enable them to meet the wants of the time. Missions encroach but feebly upon the domains of superstition and ignorance. The people are unsupplied with good public libraries. Hundreds of thousands of helpless children are growing up ignorant and vicious. Sickness and want are evermore around us. Need in a thousand forms cries for aid by a thousand voices; and while there is wealth enough in Christendom to satisfy this cry, and the cry remains unsatisfied, there will remain wrongfully withheld from its appropriate use the wealth God has sent to satisfy it. So open your hands, ye whose hands are full! The world is waiting for you! Heaven is waiting for you! The whole machinery of the divine beneficence is clogged by your hard hearts and rigid fingers. Give and spend, and be sure that God will send; for only in giving and spending do you fulfil the object of His sending.

XI.

THE LOVE OF WHAT IS OURS.

"There is one good wife in the country, and every man thinks he hath her."

"Every bird likes its own nest the best."

"Every man thinks that his own geese are swans."

WHENEVER that becomes a personal possession which is legitimately an object of love, and which involves one's character for good taste, sound judgment, and personal power or prowess, its value, in the eye and heart of its possessor, is raised above the estimate and appreciation of other minds. If we select a horse for certain points of organization, and certain characteristics of temper and training, and purchase him, we feel that, to a certain extent, that horse's reputation is a part of our own. We identify ourselves with the animal. If he trot a mile in three minutes, we are proud, as if the fact were in some way creditable to us. If he can travel eighty miles in a day, and continue it, we feel as if the fact were a compliment to ourselves. We see grandeur in the carriage of his head, and grace in the movements of his limbs, that no one else sees. So we look over our dwelling, in the arrangement and furniture of which we have expressed our best ideas of home, or into our garden, which is as we made it, and their harmony and beauty impress us as they impress no others. Our friends pass both without a thought, perhaps, or they give them a quiet compliment that means but little. Our dog may be a very ugly brute, but we own him, and do not like to hear his ugliness alluded to. We are complimented in the admiration bestowed upon the prints and paintings which adorn the walls of our parlors, quite as much as if we had made them ourselves. There are numberless beautiful and good and graceful women in the world, but that one of the number which has been the subject of our choice, and the mother of our children, is a little better than any other, although, for reasons best known to the world, we may not be the objects of any man's envy.

So it is that each man has bread to eat that the world knows not of. So it is that each man is richer than the world estimates him to be. There is more than one sense in which no man makes an honest return of his property to the assessors of taxes. All those objects of possession into which we have cast our thought, or which have come to us by a purchase involving choice and the exercise of taste and judgment, become partakers of our own life—a part of ourselves and of our own personal value. We identify all our productions with ourselves. We have a private opinion of all our literary children that no one else entertains, particularly if they are abused. Even our opinions upon the most important subjects are so recognized by us as a personal possession that we cannot separate them from our personality. It is for this reasor that political and religious conflicts are so bitter. Men do not get angry because an opinion is attacked, but because they feel themselves attacked with any opinion which they hold. Their conscience, judgment, taste—every thing in them that joined in the formation or choice of an opinion—is affronted with the attack upon the opinion itself. This is the secret of the great majority of the personalities and bitternesses that grow out of the high conflicts of opinion in the world. There is nothing to quarrel over and get excited about in an opinion, any more than in a potato, if it do not happen to belong to us. It is amusing to see the indifference with which a man will regard a public attack on an opinion which he has not accepted, and the excitement he will manifest when some cherished notion of his own is assailed.

Now, when I find a law like this running through all mankind—a law which has none but good effects when held within legitimate limits of operation—I know that it means something. Such laws are never instituted for nothing. God's benevolence is in them somewhere—that we may be sure of—and it becomes our pleasant task to find it.

The first benevolent design that shows itself to us in this law and its operation is that of making men contented and happy. If each man feel that he has got the best wife in the world, the brightest and prettiest children, the finest horse, the cleverest dog, the most convenient and tasteful home, the soundest opinions in politics and religion—that all which he possesses has advantages apparent enough to himself over the possessions of his neighbors—it is that he may be happy and contented in them. Every man may see in the peculiar pleasures which he derives from his possessions a provision of God for his special individuality—things in nature and art that answer with single and special intent to his judgment and taste, and the peculiar wants of his nature. The value that he places upon these things is not fictitious. They hold relations to him—to his nature and his wants—that they hold to no one else, and that no other things hold to him. They are, then, in a sense, a part of him. His life passes into them, and they pass into his life. He is identified with them, and they partake of those primary values which are based in each man's need of ministry.

It is in these things that we are to look for God's special manifestations of benevolence to us. We receive pleasure from the sunshine and the rain, from the stars overhead and the flowers under feet, from ocean and air, from sea and sky;—all these, in fact, are possessions—but they come to us, or are held, in common with all of our race. We are not proud of them. We do not point to the sun in vanity, nor do we boast of the nebulous silver that sheets the milky way. From the general ministry of God to the wants of the race we get no idea of His special provision for us. We see benevolence in it, but it is not meant particularly for ourselves. We find ourselves different from other men, and we find specially prepared for us those objects that arrange themselves with delightful relations around our individualities. It is not strange that they appear more valuable to us than to others, for they are, in fact, more valuable to us than to others. My friend loves devotedly a woman whom I, and perhaps no one else, could ever love at all, or love so well, and that wife is God's expression of special benevolence toward him. So is every thing which, among his possessions, has a special value in his eyes—a value not apprehended by others.

If men will examine their lot in this light, they will find themselves much richer than they generally suppose themselves to be. There is, notwithstanding the line of facts which I have developed, abundant discontent and envy in the world; and every man should look into his lot to see whether, on the whole, he would be willing to exchange it for that of any other man. Suppose that each individual who reads this article summon before his imagination the individual whose lot he has been inclined to envy. Think the matter all over, and decide, my friend, whether you would exchange places with him. Would you give up your wife, your children, your home, your associations, your sentiments and opinions, your friendships, your temptations, and your name, for his wife, children, home, associations, friendships, sentiments, opinions, temptations, and name? No? Why not? Ah! you own something too precious to surrender—you possess that wealth which is of inestimable value with relation to your own peculiar self, and which you cannot afford to exchange for any thing else under the sun. Now this wealth is the measure of God's special expression of love for you, and it is given to you to make you contented with your lot. Receive it as such, and be happy in it. Identify yourself with it. Rejoice in it, for it is something set apart by God for you, and is sacred to your use. He marries you to every one of these special blessings as truly as He marries you to the woman of your choice.

As the mind advances towards a richer life and nobler issues, another benevolent intent reveals itself as an end of this law. We dwell now among opinions, dogmas, creeds, institutions, conventionalisms, and as these lie nearest our life, we identify ourselves with them. We fight for them when they are assailed, and we are wounded in their destruction. To us they are, in certain aspects, the representatives of the will and way, the law and life of God; and it is only in moments of inspiration or exaltation that we are able to pass through, or by, these representatives, and grasp the great realities between which and our weak minds they mediate. When the soul can lay its hand on truth itself, and appropriate it; when it can say "my Lord and my God;" when it can enter sympathetically, with a rapt appreciation of the greatness and glory of its birthright, into the brotherhood of all pure intelligences; when, answering to the thrill of the blood of the Godhead in its veins, it can say "My Father;" when, with an imagination that ranges the glories of the universe, it apprehends an infinite kingdom, and sees itself a prince of the reigning house, and feels itself at home, ah! then it learns, or begins to learn, something of a law which, beginning like a rill in its humbler experiences, spreads into a river, that sweeps it into the ocean of identity with God Himself.

This is what the world, and especially the Christian world, wants to-day. It identifies itself with the shell of religion, while it needs identification with the truth, with God and His life, with all the things of God. It needs to recognize all truth as its property, God and His life as its property, and all the things of God as it property; and so to identify itself with this property that it shall feel its honor, its name, its all, bound to it —indissolubly connected with it. It was out of this thorough identification of the soul with God that came those pregnant words: "Do not I hate them that hate thee?" It is refreshing, in such a time as this, to look back upon the histories of the ancient saints, and see how closely they stood by the side of God, and bound their own personal honor to his throne. God was their God; His truth was their truth; His honor was their honor; and any attack made upon Him, His character, His truth, or His honor, was received as an attack upon themselves. We fight for our opinions, for our sect, for our church, for our institutions; they fought for Him and for His truth—for that which only gives significance and value to any institution of man. Oh! how far, how very far, are we from any just appreciation of the infinite wealth upon which we may legitimately lay our hand, as our own property! We stand and hear the name of God blasphemed with a lighter shock and a smaller draft on personal feeling than we experience when we hear a pet dogma denounced, and this simply and alone because we identify ourselves with the dogma, as our possession, mcre than we do with the Deity.

I can conceive of no reason, and I believe there is no reason, why God and Heaven, and the brotherhood of angels, seem so remote from those who believe themselves to be the sons and daughters of God, save in the fact that they have no recognized property or interest in them. The moment that these beings and things come into relation with a soul in any important sense as possessions, that soul will identify itself with them. When a soul approaches God as its Father, Heaven as its home, and all pure spirits as a portion of a family in which it rightfully holds a place, its interest and sympathy and honor are linked to them by a tie which cannot be dissolved. They enter into vital relations with its life. They enter into and become a part of its life. Its destiny is hung upon them. In short, it is identified with them in such a way that it will be wounded the most keenly and honored the most gratefully through them.

Again, the benevolence of this law, by which we identify ourselves with the things which we love as possessions, is manifested by the influence they are thus brought to bear upon our character. A man whose most highly valued possession is a horse, will so identify himself with his possession that he will rise no higher in the scale of dignity than his horse. His horse and those who are identified with a similar possession will be the best society he has. He will enjoy no other. All his talk will be horse-talk. That which holds the most intimate relation to his life will deter mine that life's development and character. Any student of human nature understands this. The class of what are strictly horse-men is just as distinctly marked a class as can be found; and its characteristics are determined by their identification with the animal to which they are devoted. The benevolence of the operation of this law may not be so apparent in this, but the operation itself is illustrated with peculiar force. As we pass on, however, to the consideration of the influence of higher possessions, we find the benevolence for which we seek.

Let God be apprehended by the soul as its own Father, and all truth as its own wealth, and all the universe as its own home—the domain of its Father—and all pure intelligences as its brethren; let all these come into the soul as possessions—as beings and things in which abide its rights and privileges—so that it identifies itself with them for time and eternity, and in the place of horse-men we have divine-men. There is no dignity in all God's world like this. It raises man above all the distinctions of wealth, above all titles, and above all earthly dignities whatsoever. It places a man where he can look up with a pure adoration. and down with a true charity. It releases him from bondage to creeds, and formularies of worship, and prescriptive lines of duty, and introduces him into the freedom of the sons of God. He is no more an alien—an outsider—a slave spurred to the performance of his task—for God's life is in him as a possession, and that life is its own law. He holds the hands of angels in his own. He lives in truth, and truth lives in him. He walks the world a prince, knowing and feeling that he is an heir of God—a joint heir with Jesus Christ. I can conceive of no dignity like this; and when I see the great world of mankind identifying itself so exclusively with its meaner possessions, content with the dignity which they confer, I see how exceedingly wide the gap is which divides the present time from the promised millennium.

Where the treasure is, there will the heart be also—the heart with all its manifestations of love, devotion, charity, and honor. I know of no good reason why the earth should differ essentially from heaven—why men may not so identify themselves with their highest treasures here that they will partake of the home feeling of those who walk in white upon the banks of the river of life—why they may not feel with relation to God and that which is most precious to Him—His children, His realm, His heaven—as they do toward their earthly father, the paternal mansion, and the brothers and sisters that cluster there.

Give us an age of gallant, chivalrous Christianity—of men who maintain the honor of their Father's house. Give us an age that shall enlist the respect of all who respect earnestness and honor. Give us an age that shall appreciate that which it is fighting for, and will not crawl before the inferior and infernal powers that make war upon the throne. Give us an age in which Christians will fight for and stand by one another, and not fight against one another. Give us an age in which Christian manhood shall assert itself as the highest earthly thing and the noblest earthly estate. Give us an age that, instead of whining and groaning under the truth, shall rejoice in the truth. Give us an age which, lifted into identity with its highest possessions, shall be made by those possessions patient, pure, heroic, and honorable. Give us the blessed thousand years!

XII.

THE POWER OF CIRCUMSTANCES.

"The straightest stick is crooked in water."
"Opportunity makes the thief."
"The orange that is too hard squeezed yields a bitter juice."
"Circumstances alter cases."

IN making up our judgments upon men and women who have fallen from their integrity, we fail to consider sufficiently the circumstances in which their fall occurred. While these may never justify the lapse which they occasioned, they furnish abundant basis for the compassionate and charitable judgment of all who, like them, are subject to temptation, and liable to circumstances that weaken the soul in its power of resistance. The straightest stick is crooked in water, and the most upright character bends, even if it do not break, when subjected to a great temptation, in circumstances that favor the wrong and tend to paralyze the power to withstand it. Before God, he or she who falls is guilty; but their fellows should be the last to point the finger of contempt, or indulge in self-righteous gratulations that they are not fallen also. It may reasonably be doubted whether, if there were to be a universal exchange of individualities in the world, the amount of sin would be sensibly diminished. In other words, if you, or I, had been subjected to the same temptations, under the same circumstances, that resulted in the sending of our old acquaintance to the state-prison for forgery, the probabilities are that we should to-day be dressing stone for the public good. If your daughter or mine had been exposed to the wiles of a villain, under the circumstances which surrounded our neighbor's daughter when she fell, and that neighbor's daughter had been in the place of ours, the probabilities are that our daughter would be lost to us and a true life, and that our neighbor's daughter would be safe. Our business, then, is to thank God for the circumstances which have favored us, to pity those who have not been thus favored, and to be very careful of our censure.

To a greater extent than the most of us imagine, the wrongs, sins and errors of the age were born of, and have been perpetuated by, circumstances. We are accustomed to inveigh against slavery. We denounce it as a high crime in those who sustain it, and a curse to all the parties concerned in it. We wonder why anybody can regard it in any different light. On the other hand, the upholders of slavery regard it as a divine institution, beneficial to the blacks and to themselves, and hold its opponents to be fanatics, hypocrites, disorganizers, and inexpressibly contemptible men. To make both parties feel more kindly toward each other, it ought to be only necessary for them to remember that, had they exchanged dwelling-places and circumstances at their birth, they would have exchanged sentiments and opinions. Our craziest abolitionists would, from their natural temperament, have been in Charleston the craziest fire-eaters, and the most zealous advocate of slavery would at the North have been the principal speaker at the Syracuse conventions. If Wendell Phillips and Lloyd Garrison had been born in New Orleans, to an inheritance of three hundred slaves apiece, and Robert Toombs and Alexander Stevens had grown up under the shadow of Bunker Hill, they would have been diametrically opposed to each other as they are to-day. It is the most senseless thing in the world for these parties to feel unkindly towards each other. Each may struggle strenuously for the maintenance of his own ideas of the right, but both should always remember that it is from no merit or demerit of theirs that they differ. Circumstances, in ninety-nine cases in a hundred, make both the opponents and the defenders of slavery.

Thus it is in the matter of religion. The Catholic regards the Protestant as no Christian, and the Protestant regards the Catholic as the upholder of the grossest errors. Each class regards the other with contempt, and wonders how it can embrace a system which it deems utterly illegitimate and fatally dangerous. What makes them differ? Circumstances, not choice. England and Ireland sit side by side, subjects of the same Queen. The English, born of Protestant parents, are Protestants. The Irish, born of Catholic parents, are Catholics. They stand in the relation of religious enemies, and talk about each other as bitterly as if they had really had something to do in making themselves what they respectively are, when, in ninety-nine cases in a hundred, they have had nothing to do with it whatever. The circumstances in which they were born and bred have made them what they are. The Catholics emigrate to this Protestant country. We regard them as misled in the main, and intentionally misleading in the exceptions. We wonder how they can pin their faith to their church in the way they do. Yet circumstances, over which they had no control, led them naturally into the Catholic church—circumstances gave them Catholic parentage, and surrounded them with Catholic influences. No Protestant can reasonably doubt that had he been born and reared under the same circumstances, he would now be a Catholic; and there are probably not ten in a thousand Catholics who would not be Protestants had they been born and bred under Protestant influences. Now, while this fact should make no difference in the estimation in which each holds the other's system of religion, it should dispossess them at once and forever of all bitterness of feeling toward each other, and of the self-righteous assumption of superiority.

It would be relevant to allude to political parties in this connection, but it is not necessary. The same fact holds good, in a general way, with relation to all the great subjects that divide men into opposing masses. It may be well, however, to say that in the matter of social position, so far, at least, as it is based in birth, there is no cause of glorying on the part of any man. Two children play together, and grow up together. One is the offspring of a man of wealth and high social standing. The other is the son or daughter of a laborer, poor, and, perhaps, ignorant. One of these children comes in time to look down upon his humble neighbor, and the other is brought to feel, sooner or later, that he is proscribed. What makes these children to differ? Nothing but circumstances, over which neither had a particle of control, yet one of them gets proud in his adventitious position—proud of his circumstances. Circumstances, ordered by Providence, doubtless, grade society through all the steps that reach from the bottom to the top of it. This fact may be recognized—all the classes of society may be recognized—and yet between each class there cannot legitimately be a particle of bitterness, of envy, of jealousy or of pride.

Again, to leave this class of generalizations, let us instance a lad in the city born of drunken parents, and trained to familiarity with the observation and the practice of vice from the earliest conscious moment of his life. He is a beggar at six, a thief at ten, a drunkard at twelve, a libertine at sixteen, and a murderer at twenty. Another lad is born in a quiet country home, with a Christian father and mother. His whole training is in the direction of virtue. As soon as he can speak, he is taught to pray. He is carefully guarded from all vicious influences, educated in the atmosphere of a pure and self-sacrificing love, becomes the possessor of a lofty Christian purpose, and, at thirty, finds himself by the side of the poor convict boy of the city, endeavoring to prepare him for the change of worlds which will come with his execution. What makes the lives of these two men differ so widely? What, but circumstances? I do not say that this city boy is, in his history, the representative of all the vicious men and women in the world, but he is, in many respects, the representative of the larger part of them, as the country boy is the representative of the larger part of the virtuous. How ought this fact to open wide the arms of our pity and our charity towards those whose steps are bent toward ruin! How inconsiderate is that self-righteous contempt and abhorrence with which a virtuous world regards those who only needed favoring circumstances to make them pure and worthy as itself.

The truth is, that the great brotherhood and sisterhood of sin groan under the uncharitable judgments of those who, but for circumstances interposed by other power than their own, would have been among their number. These judgments may not be unjust, but they are uncalled for. They may be just, coming from Him who sees the heart, but they are illegitimate, proceeding from those whom kinder circumstances have aided to preserve. I say they groan under these judgments. They feel bitterly in regard to them, and they will accept no beneficent ministry at the hands of the good until they receive the sympathy to which they believe themselves entitled. Any man who approaches this class in an attempt do them good, with censure on his ips, and the assumption of a self-won and self-preserved righteousness in his bearing, will find, to the cost of his mission, that every heart is closed against him. There is a basis of brotherhood and tender sympathy in this connection of circumstances with the development of character and life, and on this basis every man must stand who would raise the fallen, strengthen the weak, and reclaim the erring.

Leaving classes, we come to individuals. The orange that is too hard squeezed yields a bitter juice Here and there, in the path of our observation, we see men and women who, having lived good and reputable lives, yield to some sudden and overwhelming temptation, and fall with a crash that startles our hearts with terror. Some man whom, through a life of strict integrity, we have regarded as a model of honor and honesty, suddenly stands before the world condemned as a defaulter, a swindler, a forger. Did it ever occur to you to stop for a moment, and think what a band of circumstances must have conspired against, and what temptations must have assailed him, even to lead him one step towards the resistance of conscience, the sacrifice of his peace of mind, the forfeiture of his good name, and the danger of the surrender of his personal freedom? Did you ever pause in your judgment, and attempt to measure the solitary, secret, hand-to-hand conflict with the devil by which he was at last disarmed, baffled, and ruined? Did you ever attempt to realize the fact, that if you had been in his place you might have fallen like him? Do you sit coldly above the fallen man, and, with the unthinking world, condemn him? Ah! pity him; pity him. Pray that you enter not into temptation, and, while you hold his sin in horror, remember that kinder circumstances and smaller temptations have probably saved you from his fate.

Some gentle girl, full of all sweet hopes and bright with innocent beauty, gives her heart to one who is unworthy of her. She yields him her faith to be betrayed, her love to be abused, her trust to be deceived. Enslaved by circumstances, shorn of will by the blind devotion of her passion, ensnared by the toils of one whom she believes incapable of wilful wrong, she wakes from her mad dream a ruined woman. What have you to say to her, or to say about her? God forgive you, if you, man or woman, can stand over the prostrate creature from whom hope has departed, and breathe into her ears words of condemnation and scorn! Why are you, woman, who read these words, better than she? Madame, Maiden, the straightest stick is crooked in water. Condemn her sin if you will, hold it in abhorrence as you must; but when, with beseeching look, she comes into your presence, her self-righteous accusers around her, remember how the Christ that is in you impels you to delay judgment, and, while revolving the pitiful circumstances of her fall, to stoop humbly and write that judgment in the sand.

The track, upon which the train of human reformation runs, is laid in sympathy, and this sympathy can never be established so long as there exists in the heart of virtue the same feeling of hatred towards the sinner that is felt towards the sin. The world will accept and can have no Saviour who has not been tempted and been surrounded with circumstances that exhibited to him the measure of human weakness. A being must be tempted "in all points like as we are" before we can give him our hand to be led up higher. The soul that does not appreciate the power of temptation has no mission to the tempted. It is a law of the heart that it will not accept the ministry of natures that have no sympathy with it. Go the world over, and select those preachers who have the greatest power over men —power to move them in high directions, and power to attract them with strong and tender affections—and they will, without exception, be found to be those who betray hearts and experiences that show that they are sympathetic with the tempted. The exceedingly proper young men who graduate from the theological institutions, in white cravats and white complexions, are men who have little power in the world, as a general thing. The world knows at once that such men know nothing of its heart; but when it finds an earnest, Christian worker, who has passed through the fire, and exhibits the possession of what we are wont to call "human nature," it turns to him with the feeling that he has a right to teach it.

There are a great many brotherhoods in the world,

but none so large as the brotherhood of temptation and untoward circumstance. A race of beings find themselves in the world without any act of their own, in circumstances not of their own choosing—some better, some worse—and all the subjects of temptation. The riddle of life is unsolved. The meaning of their relations to that which tends to degrade them is not comprehended. Now the situation of this race is, to me, one of touching and profound interest. With a God over its head and a law in its heart that hold it to accountability, and with appetites and passions within, and circumstances and temptations without, urging, coaxing, driving it to transgression—what a spectacle is this for angels and for God! Yet here we all are, struggling, toiling, falling, rising, hoping, despairing. Now, if this great fact, of common subjection to evil influence do not give us a basis for a common sympathy, I do not know what other fact in God's world does. Doubtless the brotherhood of true Christianity is a purer tie than this, but it is less a human tie and more a divine. Doubtless the love proceeding out of a pure Christian spirit is a stronger motive of labor for the elevation of men than this sympathy, but uncoupled with it, it can accomplish but little. This brotherhood is first to be recognized; this sympathy is first to be felt, before a Christian purpose with relation to the race can be indulged with any practical effect for good.

I stand by my kind; and I thank God for the temptations that have brought me into sympathy with them, as I do for the love that urges me to efforts for their good. I hail the great brotherhood of trial and temptation in the name of humanity, and give them assurance that from the Divine Man, and some, at least, of his disciples, there goes out to them a flood of sympathy that would fain sweep them up to the firm footing of the rock of safety. I assure them that there are hearts that consider while they condemn, and pity where they may not praise—that there are those even among Christian men and women, who feel attracted toward them as they cannot feel attracted toward the self-righteous and uncharitable men and women who have named the name Ineffable, and claim a place upon the rolls of the redeemed. I can never fail to remember that whatever I possess of good, of light, of liberty, of love, has come to me mainly on the wings of circumstances, and that a greater portion of the evil, the ignorance, the bondage and the hate that I see all around me was borne to those who hold and exhibit them, by the same purveyors. I come not between God's law and man's accountability, but I take the great fact as I find it, that life, in the main, follows the line of its original lot, as a basis of sympathy on which I stand with one hand in the hand of all humanity, and the other pointing hopefully toward the stars.

XIII.

ANVILS AND HAMMERS.

"When you are an anvil, bear; when you are a hammer, strike."
"There is never wanting a dog to bark at you."
"An honest man is not the worse because a dog barks at him."
"He laughs best who laughs last."

EVERY man in the world who gives blows must take blows. Every man who occupies the position of a positive force, bearing upon the thought and life of the world, is a hammer that, more or less, must submit itself to the fulfilment of the office of an anvil. Those whom he assails, or the supporters of that which he assails, will turn up his face, and undertake to straighten their crooked nails on it, or re-fasten the rivets of their broken cisterns on it, or pound the wrinkles out of their battered opinions on it, or punish it with spiteful indentations. The perfection of art with such a man is to strike heartily when he assumes the office of a hammer, and bear bravely when he is compelled to be an anvil. Until a man becomes as good an anvil as he is a hammer, he fails to be thoroughly fitted for his work. What an indurate old anvil Martin Luther was! He smote errors and abuses and sins with blows that sent their resonant echoes through all the centuries. He was a moral sledgehammer, assailing a system that shook through all its rotten timbers; but that system and its defenders returned his assaults, and tested his resistance and endurance. The diet of Worms made an anvil of him; and the kind of steel he had in him was manifested in his reply to the friends who undertook to dissuade him from going to Worms to be hammered: "Were there as many devils in Worms as there are roof-tiles, I would on!" That was the way of Luther, the anvil.

The hammer and the anvil are the two hemispheres of every true reformer's character. They are, in fact, the two aspects of every leader, let him be never so high, or never so humble. Every man who strikes blows for power, for influence, for institutions, for the right, must be just as good an anvil as he is a hammer. If he is not, he may properly conclude that he has no very important mission in the improvement and progress of his race. If private and instituted sin, error, prejudice and wrong would be kind enough to stand quietly, and let us batter in their sides, or knock them down, reform would become a fine art, with great attractions for men of weak constitutions and gentle pedigree; but they always object to this mode of treatment; and any man who attacks them must calculate on his power of resistance, or his power to bear without flinching the blows he will receive in return. A pugilist, who is an inferior hammer, not unfrequently wins a fight, in consequence of being a superior anvil. If victory were always with the hammer the French would always be victorious; but the anvil won at Waterloo.

But the blows which a reformer receives in direct response to his own are not always the hardest things he has to bear. Many become so hardened to these that they rather enjoy them. Direct and powerful opposition is a kind of compliment to the assailing power, and demonstrates fear, or the consciousness of damage, on the part of the assailed. Every system and institution of wrong, error and sin has its defenders; but, beyond these, it has adherents and friends in multitudes, who, being unable to enter the lists as champions, resort to smaller and meaner arts of enmity. There is never wanting any number of dogs to bark at an honest man. Now this playing the part of an anvil, and being the object of the vocal demonstrations of a popular quadruped, are two very different things. Many a man can withstand the fiercest blows of an individual, who will shrink from the barking of the people. Many a man can give blows valiantly and receive them bravely, who is made very nervous and miserable by clamor about his heels, and spiteful feints at the terminal portions of his pantaloons. In fact, there is nothing which a true man cannot bear, provided he is conscious of possessing the sympathy of the people.

When a reformer utterly loses, or fails to gain, the sympathy of the people, strong indeed must be his conviction, profound indeed must be his charity, and vital must his faith and purpose be, if he can still strike lustily in their behalf. Oh! how few enter upon a career of reform, in whatever department of life, and come out of it uninjured! How few are able to battle through a lifetime with the errors and sins of society, and escape unembittered toward those whom they have endeavored to benefit! How few can close a life of self-sacrifice,—misconstrued, misrepresented and abused,—with the immortal words, welling up from a heart of love still full and overflowing, "Father, forgive them, for they know not what they do!"

I suppose that indifference to direct opposition and popular clamor, even if in some sense desirable, is impossible in a nature worthy of any good work. Every man who becomes the subject of these should, however, guard himself against the consequences to which I have alluded. Every man should guard himself against a waning faith in humanity. Moral forces move slowly, partly from their nature and the complication of their processes, and partly from the lack of social sympathy among the masses of men. The most that a reformer can hope to do in his short life is to introduce a leaven into society which shall at length work the elevation he desires to effect. He can rarely move masses to his will by the immediate exercise of power, because there are, in sympathy, no such things as masses of men. There are loosely bound aggregations of individualities, but no masses through which runs so thorough a sympathy that action upon one will be action upon all. It must be remembered that a man may apparently have all society against him, and yet be engaged in a work which will certainly and thoroughly revolutionize its opinions and habits. An air-line railroad, running straight through home-lot and garden and dwelling, through hill and valley and meadow, will throw everybody upon its course into wild confusion during the progress of its construction; and were we to sympathize with the clamor of those with whose private interests it temporarily interferes, we should unite with them in calling it a curse. But when, after long preparation, and great individual labor and sacrifice, it is completed, and the cars commence their regular trips, the abutters upon the road adapt themselves to it, reap gladly and gratefully its advantages in the appreciation of their estates, and learn to regard it as a blessing which they cannot spare.

There are many good reasons why a reformer should be slow to lose his faith in humanity. The first and most obvious is, that there is always involved in this loss the loss of faith in God and in himself. I have yet to see the first reformer who has lost his faith in men—who has become sour and bitter toward his fellows—who has not also ceased to be a religious man. The religious anniversaries in the great cities nearly always are accompanied by gatherings of men who, having exhausted their faith in their fellows, and become bankrupt in charity, meet to pour into one another's ears, and into the ears of a curious multitude, the horrid discords of their blatant infidelity. The reformer feels, too, that he comes into any general judgment of his kind. If he do not feel this fully, he at least loses faith in his power over men, and, disappointed, sinks back into fretfulness over the failure of his mission, and the miscarriage of his life.

Another reason why a reformer should be slow to lose faith in men, is because they cannot at once understand him. They have lost faith in leaders, and for good cause. Leaders have been accustomed to use them for the accomplishment of selfish purposes. Thus, when a new leader arises, it takes them a long time to become fully assured of his motives. As there are always men enough whose selfishness leads them to misconstrue these motives, it may sometimes require many years for a man to vindicate himself, and secure confidence. There is no justice in blaming the people for this cautiousness: they have been deceived too often, and would be fools were they not to exercise it. A reformer has no right to expect immediate reception into the confidence of the people. They must be satisfied of the motives of him who undertakes to lead them, measure his ability, sound the depths of his charity, and intellectually comprehend his plans before they ought to consent to be guided by him. It is no more than just to say, that every reformer who has lost his faith in men, and become embittered by the loss, proves that the judgment of the people upon his character is just. He undertook a task for which he was not fit, and the people found him out.

A stronger reason still for the preservation of faith in men, is, that the more intractable and unreasonable they may be, the greater their need of reformation, and the larger draft do they make upon faith. Faith in humanity, under divine guidance and blessing, is the hope of the world. Christianity comes to us with no compulsory processes. It has faith in itself, doubtless; but without faith in men, it would never have come, or never would have made its appeal to voluntary choice. All powers that have no faith in men act by compulsion, or by circumvention. There can be no action upon will—no motives of action presented to voluntary choice—that do not proceed upon the basis of faith in humanity. The moment we lose this faith, our efforts are paralyzed, and we turn railers and accusers. A man who desires to benefit his fellows cannot proceed a single step without faith in those whom he would benefit. No matter how bad men may be, there must be, on the part of him who would reform them, the faith that there is that in them which will respond to the truth when it can be brought into contact with their judgment and conscience, or he can do absolutely nothing.

The people owe a duty to all who come to them with the professed wish to do them good. A man is not necessarily bad because a dog barks at him, and an honest man is never the worse because a dog barks at him. If you will look over your town, your state, your country, you will readily select the names of those against whom there is more or less of popular clamor. You will recall here and there names that are names of reproach. You shrink from association with those who bear them. If you enter their presence, you enter suspiciously, as if you feared a taint, or guiltily, as if you thought them conscious of the contempt in which you hold them. You think, because there is so much outcry against them, there must be something bad in them.

Now, no considerate, generous man will join in this outcry, or allow it to prejudice him against its object. It is, I believe, the general rule, that these men are men of power—of genuine progressive ideas—men who have an errand of good to their race.

Look back over the past, and see how many of those whom the world once abused are the world's idols. Who are the preachers whom you most delight to hear? Have they not, at some time in their history, been the objects of the world's outcry, and of yours, too? Look at the ballots which you carry to the polls with confidence, and perhaps with unlimited enthusiasm. Do they not bear the names of men whom you once verily believed to be the incarnations of selfishness and demagogism? Think of the statesmen, hunted to their graves by the hounds of popular clamor, who are now enthroned among the nation's immortals. Remember all the men against whom you have joined in denunciation, and whom you have learned to respect, if not to love, by getting near to them, and obtaining a look into their honest hearts and a vision of their devoted lives. Look over the whole track of history, and see how every one who ever did great good in the world has been the object of the world's maledictions, and then be careful how you join in an unreasoning outcry against any man.

While the world should be more careful and considerate in its treatment of those who come to it with a mission of good, the reformer himself should be very patient with the world. He must not only retain his faith in it, but he must not be in too great a hurry to be understood and accepted. He must draw close to the world, where it can look into his heart, and the world should draw close to him, until it is rationally satisfied that he has nothing for it. The efforts of opposing forces, backed by the indorsement of the unreasoning multitude, should throw no worker for the world off his poise, nor should they deprive him of the honest judgments of those who think. No true man will ever be in haste to vindicate himself before the world by direct efforts for that end. He has faith in men, and that gives him faith in the ultimate judgments of men. He lives, and speaks, and acts, and he is content to let his life, his words, and his actions speak for him. By them he knows that, sooner or later, the world will judge him, and he is content. Show me a man who gets excited and uneasy under popular clamor, and betrays his unhappiness and anxiety by frequent private or public explanations and justifications, and you will show me one who is not to be trusted. He has not the spirit nor the stamina for his work. But he who goes straight forward, confident in his own motives, true to his own convictions, and calmly trustful of the ultimate issue of his efforts and his life, is of the true metal, and one may be sure that there is something good in him.

He laughs best who laughs last. The wheels of progress do not stop. The world advances toward and into a better life, and will advance until, leaving the hard, clumsy and jarring pavements of the marts of selfishness behind, it will strike off joyously into the broad avenue of the millennium. No man can be a true worker for human good who does not believe that the cobble-stone pavement has an end, and that there is an avenue ahead where it will be his turn to enjoy himself. He believes that the time will come when what he is doing, and has done, will be accepted at its true value. He may be laughed at now; he may be scoffed at and scorned; his motives may be maligned; he may be hammered by opposition and barked at by popular clamor; but he knows that sometime in the future it will be his turn to laugh, and he is confident that he will laugh last and laugh best. He knows that God will prove to be a good paymaster, and he believes that the world will, in the long run, be just.

If any man propound ideas in advance of the world, the world, in its progress, will come up to them, as certainly as the world continues to exist, and then, if not before, it will remember. Those who cherish truth and stand by the right, must be at warfare with those who hold to falsehood and to sin. There is no conscription in this war. It is a voluntary service on both sides, and neither is in want of cowards. There is a contemptibly quiet path for all those who are afraid of the blows and clamors of opposing forces. There is no honorable fighting for any man who is not ready to forget that he has a head to be battered and a name to be bespattered. Truth wants no champion who is not as ready to be struck, as to strike, for her. The eye that can see the triumph of that which is good in the world from afar, the heart that can be certain of victory, though now in the sulphurous thickness of the fight, can afford present contumely and even present defeat. The bearer of such a heart and eye knows that, sooner or later, the time will come when he and the band to which he belongs shall celebrate a final victory over all that oppose them—that they shall come home from the contest "with songs and everlasting joy upon their heads." He knows that the last shout will be his, and that the severer the conflict the heartier will that shout be. Ah! what peans of triumph, what sweeps of majestic music, what waving of banners, what joyous tumult of white-robed hosts, shall greet him who goes home, worn and weary, to take a crown worthily won in the contest with error and with wrong. May that crown be yours and mine!

XIV.

EVERY MAN HAS HIS PLACE.

"You stout and I stout,
Who shall carry the dirt out?"
"Every man cannot be vicar of Bowden."
"He that cannot paint must grind the colors."

WHO shall be vicar of Bowden and who shall carry the dirt out—who shall paint and who shall grind the colors—are questions which, in various forms, have agitated the world since human society existed. Dissatisfaction with position and condition is well nigh universal. Every man walks with his eyes and wishes upwards—some moved by aspiration for a nobler good, others by ambition for a higher place; some by emulation of a worthy example, others by discontent with the allotments of Providence. The infant does not forget to climb when he learns to walk, nor is the man less a climber than the boy. Every thing is towering, or climbing, or reaching, or looking upward. The elm stretches its feathery arms and waves its hands toward the clouds that hang over it; the vine pulls itself up the elm by its delicate fingers; and the violet sits at the foot of the vine and looks up, and breathes its fragrant wishes heavenward. Even the sleeping lakelet in the meadow dreams of stars, and will not be satisfied without a private firmament of water-lilies. It is as if God had whispered into the ear of all existence, the moment it was emerging from nhility, the words—"look up!" and, hardly knowing why, it had been looking up ever since. Well, this is right; for, far above every thing shines the great White Throne—sits the Father Soul—abide the treasuries of all good—burns the uncreated fire at which the torches of life were lighted. It is a natural, instinctive thing to look upward.

Discontent may be a very good thing, or a very bad thing. There is a discontent which is divine,—which has its birth in the highest and purest inspirations that visit and stir the soul. All that discontent which grows from dissatisfaction with present attainment, or springs from a desire for higher usefulness, or has its birth in motives that impel to the worthy achievement of an honorable name and an honorable place, is a thing to be visited by blessings and benisons. Discontent which comes from below—which comes from a soul disgusted with its lot—a soul faithless in

God, and out of harmony with the arrangements and the operations of Providence, is an evil thing—only evil—and that continually. One holds the principle of love; the other of malice. One is attracted from above; the other is instigated from below. One tends to the development of a symmetrical, strong, and harmonious character; the other to disorganization and depreciation. One is from heaven, the other is from hell.

I look out of my window, and see a carriage rolling by, with its freight of richly-dressed ladies. On the coach-box sits a man who drives the horses when they go, and opens the door of the carriage and lets down the steps when they stop. Further up the street there is a building going up. The architect stands by with his hand in his breast, giving directions. The hod-carrier, smeared with mortar, passes him, climbs the giddy ladder, and drops the bricks upon the scaffolding, and these, one after another, are driven to their places by the ringing trowel of the brick-layer. I rise from my seat, and walk through the rooms adjoining my own. Here sits an editor, hastily putting together the thoughts that will form to-morrow's leader. At another table sits another editor, culling from a pile of exchanges bits of intelligence that come in on a thousand paper wings from other communities. At their cases stand the compositors, setting up, type by type, the matter which the editors prepare for them. The pressman and the engineer have their respective parts to perform. I find the great aggregate of life to be a network of duties—an organized system of duties. In order to secure the comfort of the whole, there is a certain amount of work to be done, infinitely various in kind. There must be an architect to plan, there must be a hod-carrier to bear mortar, and a brick-layer to lay the bricks, or we shall have no buildings. There must be an editor, and a compositor, and a pressman, or there will be no newspaper. Who shall do the thinking, and who shall perform the manual labor? Who shall paint, and who shall grind the colors? Every man cannot be vicar of Bowden.

It does not suffice to tell discontented people that every man has his place, and will find his highest account in seeking to fill it, and to fill it well. What particularly troubles them is, that they were made for so low a place. They really call God's wisdom and benevolence in question for assigning to them subordinate offices in operating the machinery of society. A man finds himself distinguished by clumsy hands and broad shoulders, with a hod on his back, and complains that he was not made for a brick-layer; and the brick-layer wishes he had the ease and the honor of the architect, and wonders why his power of achievement is so closely circumscribed. The coachman rubs down his horses, and marvels that he was not born to their ownership, and that the owner was not born to drive for him. So people quarrel with their position, the world over. Every thing in the world is unequal to these people. They do not see the impartial justice of conferring upon one man great mental faculties, pleasant address, and commanding presence, while another is condemned to be a dwarf, both in mind and body, and to serve his more highly-favored neighbor that he may win bread and raiment.

Well, there is all this work to do: who shall do it? A link broken in the chain will spoil the chain. There are all these places to fill: who shall fill them? I fill a subordinate office in the world: why should not you? Is there any good reason why you should be vicar of Bowden, and the vicar of Bowden should tend a toll-bridge, or conduct a railroad train? Since these things are to be done by somebody, you and I may as well take the part that comes to us, and perform it. It is not best to stop the wheels of society on our private account. If you and I have had any injustice done to us in the assignment of our duties, it will not mend any thing to fasten our ill-fortune upon somebody else; and you and I are not the men to skulk, I think. Genuine, manly pluck and good nature will settle much of this difficulty. If our advance involve nothing more than a change of places with others, it is not exactly the manly thing to whine about our lot.

But there is a better and a broader basis for the settlement of this matter than this; and did we possess even a modicum of the faith in God that we ought to possess, we should feel certain there would be such a basis, though we might fail to find it. The instinctive, persistent search of the soul is for happiness. We seek for office, or place, or wealth; we pine over the fact that our mental endowments and acquisitions are comparatively indifferent or positively mean; and why? Because, while we lie dreaming upon our pillow of stone, the places and positions of life shape themselves into a ladder on which angels ascend and descend, the last round leaning on a heavenly landing; because that which is above us, in allotment, gift, and acquisition, forms so many steps of the gradatory that leads from the cells where we do penance, to the temple where we expect peace and heavenly communion. In other words, we are discontented because we believe there is more happiness on the upper steps of society than on ours; and here is where the great mistake is made.

If there be any thing which human history teaches more thoroughly than any other thing—if there be any fact revealed to observation more clearly than any other fact—it is, that happiness does not depend upon condition and position—that it has its birth in possessions and relations superior to, and in most respects unaffected by, those facts of individual and social life which divide men into classes. Here is where the Good Father equalizes human lot. High position, considered by itself, is not a positive good—is not, in and of itself, a source of happiness to the souls planted upon it. There is no good reason to be found in the whole universe of God why the coachman should not be as happy as the dainty ladies whom he serves. There is no reason why the hod-carrier may not be as happy as the bricklayer, and the bricklayer as happy as the architect. Wants keep pace with wealth always. Responsibility walks hand in hand with capacity and power. Of him to whom much is given much will be required. Posts of honor are evermore posts of danger and of care. Each office of society has its burden, proportioned to its importance ; so that men shall find no apology for murmuring at the better lot of their neighbors, while all are made dependent for happiness upon common sources—open alike to him who wears fine linen and fares sumptuously every day, and the beggar who waits at his gate.

I am inclined to think that if our minds were capable of apprehending the essential facts of the life we see, we should be convinced that happiness is one of the most evenly distributed of all human possessions. The laborer loves his wife and children as well as the lord, and takes into his soul all the tender and precious influences that flow to him through their love as well as he. Food tastes as sweetly to the ploughman as the placeman. If the latter have the daintier dish, the former has the keener appetite. Into all ears the brook pours the same stream of music, and the birds never vary their programme with reference to their audiences. The spring scatters violets broadcast, and grass grows by the roadside as well as in the park. The breeze that tosses the curls of your little ones and mine is not softer in its caresses of those who bound over velvet to greet it. The sun shines, the rain falls, the trees dress themselves in green, the thunder rolls, and the stars flash, for all alike. Health knows nothing of human distinctions, and abides with him who treats it best. Sleep, the gentle angel, does not come at the call of power, and never proffers its ministry for gold. The senses take no bribes of luxury; but deal as honestly and generously by the poor as by the rich; and the President of the United States would whistle himself blind before he could call our dog from us.

If we examine this matter critically, we shall find that the sweetest satisfactions that come to us are those which spring from sources common to the race. If you and I are worthy men, that which is most precious to us, as the material of our daily happiness, is precisely that which is not dependent upon the positions we respectively occupy in the world. Now, if we look above this range of common Providence into that realm of fact, in which abides our common relationship to a common Father, the distinctions of society and the variety and contrariety of human lot fade away and become contemptible. If God smile on me and fill my heart with peace; if He forgive my sin, and give me promise and assurance of a higher life beyond the grave; if He call me His child, and draw out from my cold and selfish heart a filial love for Him; if He inspire me with a brotherly charity that embraces in its arms all who bear His image; if He give me a hope more precious to me than all gold, and transform the narrow path in which I walk into the vestibule of Heaven, it will very naturally be a matter of indifference to me whether I paint, or grind the colors—whether I carry dirt, or officiate as the vicar of Bowden. If we were all made in His image; if we are all held amenable to the same law; if we all have offer of the same salvation; if we are all to be judged according to our deeds; if we have the promise of the same heaven on the same terms, it shows, at least, what God thinks of human distinctions.

The ministry of nature, and love, and sympathy, are common to all men. On the broad platform of morals, the king stands uncovered by the side of the peasant, and wealth and place flaunt no titles and claim no privileges. In religion, all men kneel and worship a common Lord. Men are placed in different positions in this world simply because there is a great variety of work to do, and no one man can do all kinds. If you and I have found our places—if we find ourselves engaged in doing that thing which, on the whole, we can do better than any thing else, then low discontent with our lot is not only sinful but mean. God gives to you and to me just as many sources of innocent happiness as he has given to anybody, and opens to us just as fair a heaven as he has opened to anybody. It becomes us, therefore, to fill our places, and do our particular duties well, hold up our heads in front of every man with self-respectful complacency, do honor to the office which God has selected for us, by a faithful performance of its functions, and take and pocket contentedly the penny a day which we get in common with others. The Creator doubtless knew what weak, unreasonable, and inconsistent creatures we should be when he made us; but if you and I had made a world full of people, and set them at work with pledge of even pay and equal privilege in all essential good, and they had set themselves to erecting artificial distinctions among themselves, and gone to whining over the parts we had assigned to them, we should be exceedingly disappointed, not to say disgusted.

Still, we may all look up. There are steps to be

climbed in life, but we can only climb them worthily by becoming fit for the ascent. It is only after becoming prepared for important places, through the education involved in the intelligent and faithful discharge of the duties of the place in which we find ourselves, that it is best, or even proper, that we be advanced. It is not those who pine and whine, and quarrel with their lot, who are apt to change it for one which the world calls better. Aspiration, worthy ambition, desire for higher good for good ends—all these indicate a soul that recognizes the beckoning hand of the Good Father who would call us homeward toward himself—all these are the ground and justification of a Christian discontent; but a murmuring, questioning, fault-finding spirit has direct and sympathetic alliance with nothing but the infernal. So while God gives you and me the privilege of being as happy as any other man, and makes us responsible for nothing more than he gives us, let us be contented, and,

"Still achieving, still pursuing,
Learn to labor and to wait."

XV.

INDOLENCE AND INDUSTRY.

"Idleness is the sepulchre of a living man."
"Constant occupation prevents temptation."
"Idle men are the Devil's play-fellows."
"Business is the salt of life."

HUMANITY is constitutionally lazy. I have yet to see the first child take naturally to steady work, or the first young man look forward with no desire to an age of ease. There are multitudes of men who love work, but they have learned to love it, and have learned that they are made truly happier by it. We are all looking forward to some golden hour when we may "retire from business," read the newspapers at leisure, drive a pair of steady bay horses, walk to the post-office with a well-fed belly and a gold-headed cane, and be free. I do not believe that any man ever became thoroughly industrious, save under the impulsion of motives outside of the attractions of labor. We labor, because it is necessary for us to labor for sustenance, or to achieve an object of ambition, or because idleness is felt to be a greater evil than labor. The number of potatoes unearthed in the world "for the fun of it," would not feed a flock of sheep. In fact, I believe that God made us lazy for a purpose. He did not intend that we should have any thing but air and water costless. If labor were a pleasure, we should have really to pay for nothing, and, as a consequence, we should prize nothing that we have. All values have their basis in cost, and labor is the first cost of every thing on which we set a price. But labor has a higher end than this, and I will try to reveal it.

Every man and woman is born into the world with a stock of vitality which must be expended in some way. It may be breathed out in unnecessary sleep, or appropriated wholly to the digestion of unnecessary food, and a good deal of it runs to waste in these ways. It may be expended in sport and in play, it may be exhausted in sickness, or it may be applied to labor. This vitality is naturally a restless principle. In the boy, to whom existence is fresh, we find it unchained, and betraying itself in antics and races, and foolhardy feats, and various play. It impels him to exercise and activity in all places and at all times. This vitality is alike the basis of mental and muscular power. Forth from it proceeds all action whatsoever. When we possess it, we live; when it leaves us, we die.

This vitality is, then, the matrix, as it is the measure, of inherent power; yet one man with a given stock of vitality may have a hundred times the practical power of another man whose stock of vitality is the same, the reason being that the organs of action, through which vitality manifests itself, and by which it works, are better trained in one case than in the other. Use is the condition of development of all the powers of the body and the soul. Facility of action comes by habit. A man from any outside profession, obliged to write a daily brace of leaders for the newspaper, would break down in six months, while the accustomed editor would not find himself fatigued beyond his wont. The greatest mind in the nation would find itself perplexed and exhausted in the attempt to make a horse-shoe, while some humble apprentice of the smithy would make one of superior excellence with comparative ease. The greater the facility that may be acquired in the use of organs and faculties, the smaller the draft will be upon the vitality that feeds them. The reason why some men accomplish so much more than others is not, generally, that they have more vitality than others, but that the facility of labor which use and habit have given them enables them to do more without vital exhaustion.

Now life means but little unless it means that we are in a state of education—a condition in which our powers and faculties are to be educed. If we are not in training for something, this life is one of the most serious of all practical jokes. Labor in all its variety, corporeal and mental, is the instituted means for the methodical development of all our powers, under the direction and control of will. Through the channels of labor this vitality is to be directed. Into practical results of good to ourselves and others it is all to flow, and those results will prescribe the method which we need. It is to secure this great end of development that the prizes of life are placed before us as things to be worked for. When we get these prizes, they seem small; and, intrinsically, they are of but little value. They are, in fact, little better than diplomas that testify of long labor, worthily performed. Still before us rises worthier good, to stimulate us to harder labor and higher achievement. Still the will urges on the organs of the body and the faculties of the mind till that habit which is second nature gives them the law of action, and employment itself becomes its own exceeding great reward.

Still, the most industrious of us feel, at times, that we are laboring by compulsion. Often both the spirit and the flesh are unwilling and weak. We are goaded to labor by need. We are urged to labor because we cannot enjoy our leisure. We labor because we are ashamed to be idle. Many a man, bowed down by his daily toil, looks forward to the grave for rest; and far be it from me to tell him that he is looking and hoping for that which he will never experience. I do not believe there will be any hurry in eternity, or any such necessity of labor as we have here. If I have a competent comprehension of the spiritual estate, it will tax us but little for food and clothing; and if the labor to which we devote ourselves here shall train us to facility in the use of our powers, the work that will be given to us to do there will be something to be grateful for. We shall have all the rest we want. A sleep of a century will make no inroads upon our time, if we need any such sleep. But I have an idea that when the clogs are off, and the old feeling of youth comes back, we shall be glad to have something to do, and that the use of powers which labor has trained under the direction of will for worthy ends will be everlasting play, as keenly enjoyed as the play of the restless boy.

It is only as we look upon labor in this light that we understand its real value and significance. If the prizes we win here are all the reward that labor brings, it pays but poorly. But labor, like all the passages through which God would lead our life, is full of incidental rewards. The man who carves the channel of a laborious life, taps the springs of tribu:ary joys through every mile. Health is an incident of powers well trained and industriously employed. Self-respect wells up in the heart of him whose energies, under the con trol of his will, are directed to worthy ends. Popular regard crowns him who is a worthy worker. The sleep of the laboring man is sweet, and none but he knows the luxury of fatigue. Temptation flies from the earnest and contented laborer, and preys upon the brain and heart of the idler. Labor brings men into sympathy with the worthy men of the world. So, there is enough of joy to be found in labor, if we will only mark its source, to encourage and content us, even if the great end of labor be somewhat hidden from us, as it doubtless is from multitudes of men.

This vitality of which I have been talking will find vent somewhere. If, under the direction of the will, it is not taxed for the support of methodical labor, it will demonstrate its nature in irregular ways. Wherever we find a profession or calling, excellence in which demands great vital power, and exercise in which taxes that vital power but little, or only for brief periods of time, there we shall find vitality seeking demonstration through the passions. No person can be a great singer, a great actor, a great orator, or a great writer without great vitality. In the case of the singer, the actor and the orator this vitality, absolutely necessary for great success, is only subject to draft on occasions. In the lives of all these people there are long intervals of repose, in which the unused energies seek expenditure. As a natural consequence, they are subject to great temptations, and their lapses from virtue are notorious. I would traduce no class of persons in the world. There are among these classes as pure and noble men and women as are to be found in any class, and the purer and nobler because their virtue costs them something. There is always something peculiarly dangerous in a calling that requires great vitality at irregular intervals; and the followers of such callings should understand the philosophy of their danger, and guard themselves with peculiar care.

This will illustrate very well the influence of idleness upon the morals. There are those in the world upon whose vitality labor makes no draft whatever. They are not subject even at intervals to legitimate expenditures of vitality; but they have it, and, unless impotent in will or imbecile in passion, that vitality will have expenditure. No truly Christian man can be truly an indolent man. He must necessarily have established legitimate channels of methodical, vital expenditure, or his Christianity will be a very weak affair. There is really nothing left to a genuine idle man, who possesses any considerable degree of vital power, but sin. A man who has nothing to do is the devil's play-fellow. He has no choice in the matter. He can find no sympathy anywhere else. Good men find nothing in him congenial. Industrious men have no time to devote to him, and would have no sympathy with him if they had. All the decent world is in league against an idle man. Everybody despises him, whether he be rich or poor. Everybody feels that he is a nuisance—that he is a sneak, who refuses to employ the powers with which he has been endowed, and declines to contribute his quota to the support of the race. He is driven by the very necessity of his position into secret or open vice, and he finds in obedience to the calls of temptation the only delights that season an otherwise insipid life.

Idleness is the sepulchre of a living man. A man whose will refuses to direct the vitality within him into regular channels of labor—who simply feeds and sleeps, or nurses his passions and his appetites—whose highest satisfaction comes from sense—is as good as dead and buried. Of what use is such a man in the world, to himself or others? If he will not work, he is a burden upon society, even if he prey upon a pile of inherited wealth. That wealth, if he were out of the way, would pass into better hands; and the world has need of it for its workers. No man has a right to be idle if he can get work to do, even if he be as rich as Crœsus, simply because he cannot be an idle man without injury to himself and to society. He destroys his own happiness, buries his powers of usefulness, and furnishes to the world a pestilent example.

If any rich young man read these words, I have something of importance to say to him. Your father, either by business enterprise or family inheritance, is rich. You know the amount of his wealth, and you know there is enough of it to support you while you live, without labor. Here is a great temptation. As I have said before, humanity is constitutionally lazy; and when you see how severely the prizes of life are to be struggled for, you naturally shrink from the sharp, and, what seems to be, the unnecessary competition. There is also, perhaps, in your mind, a prejudice against labor. It may not appear to you a very genteel thing to tie yourself to a daily round of duties. You like to be independent, and to show that you are so. Now be very careful here, or you will make the great mistake of your life—a mistake which some day you will be willing to give all your wealth to recall. I know that you cannot be happy without fulfilling the end of your being, and so do you. I know that you cannot fulfil the end of your being without the thorough development of your powers by the regular, systematic expenditure of your vitality in labor. I know that unless you do this, time will be left upon your hands to be dreamed away alone, or inflicted as a bore upon others who have something to do, or to be filled up by ministry to appetites which will degrade you. So I say to you, never dream, for a moment, of a life of idleness. Such a life will curse you and injure others. Such a life is as unmanly as it is ungodly. It has no redeeming feature and no apology. Have a profession, or a calling, of some kind, which shall make a regular tax upon your powers. Only in this way can you be reasonably safe from low temptations, acquire self-respect, secure the esteem of men, and place yourself in sympathy with this working world.

I know that there are many who are obliged to work too hard—whose vitality is taxed beyond measure, and beyond the profit of the organs and faculties by which it is expended. While this fact is partly owing to the multiplicity and extravagance of artificial wants, it might be greatly modified by a more universal adoption of the habit of labor. The burdens of the world are unequally borne. A great multitude live without labor; they are drones in the hive. A still greater multitude live by their wits; and over all this country—never more than at the present time—is there a disposition to gain wealth out of the regular channels of business. The real "English" of this mode of acquiring wealth is to get it without earning it—a way of legally gaining possession of what others have earned by the sweat of their brows. Nearly all the popular modes and means of speculation are modes and means of legal gambling. Not a dollar is produced in the world that is not either taken from the ground, or pulled from the sea by somebody; and it is a shameful fact, that the popular means of winning wealth contemplate its acquisition without a particle of labor bestowed upon its production. I do not believe that wealth won in this way is the right way. There is a legitimate business of mediation between producers and consumers, and a legitimate line of service to both, but further than this, all those who seek for wealth without adding a grain to the general stock, are leeches, sponges, nuisances.

There is a more honorable way. There are legitimate offices of service to the world for which the world will pay well; and, in one of these, at least, every man should have a place, and there do the work of his life, winning competence as he will, and wealth if he may. Wealth, legitimately acquired, is valuable, and it is only valuable when thus acquired. Honest labor for the world is the only true basis of wealth, and the grand pre-requisite for its enjoyment. I have said that everybody looks forward to the time when he can retire from business. There may be something in this beyond the the natural laziness of men, or their desire for ease. It may be that some intuition of the soul overleaps its earthly life, and, seeing the heavenly goal but dimly, plants its reward of labor on this side the river, when it should be placed among the gardens upon the other bank. Be that as it may, retiring from business has most commonly proved a disastrous operation.

There are old men and old women whose work of life is really done, and who may in peace and content sit down and wait their mysterious transit. We love these weary workers, and bid them be happy. But a man who retires from business before the work of life is done, in the full possession of his powers, retires from happiness and health. His stock of vitality is unexpended; and uneasy and discontented must his life be, unless that vitality find an outlet through legitimate channels. A life of active business carves deep channels, and it is very hard to change them. Better far to die in the old harness than to try to put on another. But all may look forward to an age of leisure, lying in the unknown land, where powers, trained to ease of action by labor, will find themselves fed by a vitality immortal as that in which abide the springs of all power.

XVI.

THE SINS OF OUR NEIGHBORS.

"You have daily to do with the Devil, and pretend to be frightened at a mouse."

"Don't measure other people's corn by your own bushel."

THERE is little in the conduct and condition of men that is not the subject of a false valuation; and I can imagine nothing, save larger hearts and more plentiful brains, that would be of so much use to the world as a catalogue of sins, arranged upon an intelligible scale, so that their comparative enormity might be settled at a glance. Such a catalogue might serve a good purpose, generally, perhaps, by pointing out the real sinners of the world, and thus bringing the materials of society to their true level; but its chief benefits would inure to those who are in the habit of over-estimating their own virtues, under-estimating their own vices, attaching fictitious importance to the sins of others, and clothing in the crimson of crime acts and practices as harmless and sinless as the prattle of children, as well as to those who

"Compound for sins they are inclined to,
By damning those they have no mind to."

There are men, for instance, who attach a peculiar merit to the entertainment of a certain set of theological opinions—who entertain those opinions very decidedly, and maintain them wonderfully well, while they make dissent an absolute sin, and regard dissenters with pity and contempt. There are men who judge their neighbors with great uncharitableness; who drive hard bargains; who gamble in stocks; who are self-righteous and censorious; who fail in tenderness toward God's poor; who never pay what they ought to pay for the support of the religious institutions to which they are attached, yet who would consider a social dance in their own parlor a terrible sin, and a game of whist a high crime that should call down the judgments of Heaven. There are men who stalk about the world gloomy, and stiff, and severe—self-righteous embodiments of the mischievous heresy that the religion of peace and good-will to all mankind—the religion of love, and hope, and joy—the religion that bathes the universal human soul in the light of parental love, and opens to mankind the gates of immortality—is a religion of terror—men guilty of misrepresenting Christ to the world, and doing incalculable damage to his cause, yet who find it in them to rebuke the careless laughter that bubbles up from a maiden's heart that God has filled with life and gladness.

This fallacious estimate of the respective qualities and magnitudes of sins has not only blinded the reason and befooled the conscience of the world, but it has spoiled its language by parallel processes of exaggeration and emasculation. Little words, that legitimately represent little things, have become monstrous words, representing monstrous things. Great sins have pleasant words attached to them, which serve as masks by which they find their way into good society without suspicion. Individual notions—no bigger than a man's hand, at first—have spread themselves into overshadowing ecclesiastical dogmas. Phrases have been invested by the schools with illegitimate meanings and deceptive sanctity. The age is an age of words, and is ruled by words rather than things; and there is hardly one of them that has not shrunk from its original garments, or outgrown them. Men are saved by words, and damned by words. Religion rides the nominal and casuistry the technical; and the unfortunate wight who does not get out of the way will be crushed by words, or run through by a fatal phrase.

The religious newspapers of the day are full of

quarrels about words—quarrels instituted in the name of the Prince of Peace, and carried on for the benefit of the Prince of Darkness—quarrels over non-essential matters of opinion—quarrels growing out of rivalries of sects—quarrels fed by the fires of human passion—quarrels maintained by the pride of opinion and by the ambition for intellectual mastery—quarrels whose only tendency is to disgust the world with the religion in whose behalf they are professedly instituted, and to fret, and wound, and divide the followers of Jesus Christ. Yet these same religious papers will deplore the personal collision of two drunken congressmen in the streets of Washington as a sad commentary on the degeneracy of the age, and moralize solemnly over a dog-fight. They can lash each other with little mercy—they can call each other names, abuse each other's motives, misconstrue each other's language, criminate and recriminate, but faint quite away with seeing a cart-horse over-whipped, or a race-horse over-tasked. They have daily to do with the devil, and pretend to be frightened at a mouse.

What is true of the controversial religious newspapers, is true, I fear, of a great many Christian men and women. They have pet sins—poodle sins—with silky white hair—sins held in by a social collar and a religious ribbon—that bark at good honest dogs, or imaginary dogs, although their little eyes are red with the devil that is in them. As sectarians, they are given to slander. They speak disparagingly of those who differ with them in belief. They judge uncharitably those who engage in practices which only their particular dictionary makes diabolical. They blacken a multitude of good deeds by dipping them into bad motives of their own steeping. Now, if I were called upon to decide which, in my opinion, is the least sinful in itself, and the least demoralizing in its tendency—the traducing of one of Christ's disciples by another of Christ's disciples, or engaging in or witnessing a horse-race—I should turn my back on the traducer and shake hands with the jockey.

I know men not religious, who bear about an exceedingly sensitive idea of honor that scorns all littleness and meanness and trickery—chivalrous men—reliable men—men really of pure lives and honest and honorable impulses—yet men so warped in their reason and their moral nature that they will follow their party leaders through all the treacheries, perjuries, and innominable rascalities that party leaders, driven to desperate straits, can invent; who stand squarely up to the endorsement of deceit, injustice, robbery, and murder; who pamper and patronize the most brutal and dangerous elements of society, and who give money to be used for party purposes that they have no reasonable doubt will be directed to the corruption of the ballot-box. I know women of delicate instincts and really modest natures who turn the cold shoulder to a fallen sister—passing her with a shuddering sense of pollution—yet who gladly associate with, and even marry, men who are notorious for their infamous gallantries—yielding to the salute of the seducer the lip that curled with scorn in the presence of his victim.

I have dealt thus far in matters of fact. They are patent; everybody apprehends them. I will go still further in these matters of fact, and declare that it may be recorded, as a rule pretty universally reliable, that a man or woman who is particularly severe upon the minor sins of mankind—who lacks compassion for the fallen, and consideration for the weak and tempted—carries, nine times in ten, a large sin, with a little name, in the sleeve. Those who see much to find fault with in others, and who are prone to magnify and dwell upon the shortcomings of their neighbors, are those who have an interest in depreciating the life and character around them. Men do not work for nothing. They work for pay; and when I see one who seems particularly desirous of depreciating others, I know it is only for the purpose of bringing them down to the mean standard which he is conscious measures his own life.

Is this uncharitable? I think not. Is it not always the purest woman who is the last to suspect impurity in other women, the most unwilling to believe ill of her neighbor, the first charitably to palliate the offences of those who fall, and the first to give them the hand of sympathy? Is not the Christ within them always saying—"Neither do I condemn thee; go, and sin no more?" Is it not always the noblest man who deals the easiest with the foibles of his neighbor? Is it not always the best man who is busiest with looking after his own sins, and who has neither time nor disposition to discover and denounce those of others? Is it not always the most Christlike Christian who esteems others better than himself, and who modestly regards his own heart as altogether untrustworthy? I think so.

"Who art thou that judgest another man's servant?" Who gave you authority to measure other people's corn by your particular bushel? Who gave you liberty to thrust forward your fallible judgment, your warped and weak reason, your little notions, your uncharitable heart, your long and lathy creed, and your rule of life taken at second hand, and badly damaged at that—as the standard of the great world's life? Why will you be always sallying out to break lances with other people's wind-mills, when your own is not capable of grinding corn for the horse you ride? Doubtless the world is wicked enough, but it will not be improved by the extension of a spirit which self-righteously sees more to reform outside of itself than in itself. Doubtless there are great sins, practiced by multitudes of men, but they will hardly be diminished by those who bring into the enterprise of extermination a greater amount of baggage than they can defend.

It so happens, in the great economy of life, that there is but one thing by which men may legitimately be judged; and that is the heart. It so happens, also, that only the Being who made it is capable of judging it. If we are determined to measure every thing developed by the life around us by our own bushel, let us first of all go to the divine standard, and get our bushels "sealed." Let us endeavor to apprehend something of the infinite love which flows out unmeasured from the Father's heart to every creature proceeding from the Father's hand. Let us recognize that essential fact in the human constitution which renders uniformity of belief and faith with relation to all truth, and identity of action from identity of motive, impossible.

There are no twin souls in God's universe. Each stands alone in its relation to each particular truth within the range of its apprehension. In the field of life, each has its standpoint, from which it observes, and at which it receives impressions from all the facts, persons, and phenomena of the field. This round world of ours rolls ceaselessly in the sea of light poured from the exhaustless fountains of the sun. All around it, thick strewn with stars, bends the blue firmament. It seems to every man as if he were standing in the centre of the world. The heaven that swells above him, skirted by a horizon that may be narrow or broad, is the true heaven. The constellated lights that rise and set upon his vision have relation to him as a kind of sentient centre. That which is up, is necessarily above his head, where his sun shines and his moon sails; that which is down is beneath his feet; and he can hardly conceive why his antipodes do not die of apoplexy, or drop out of the system of things into the ethereal abyss. So this world of human life revolves, a perfect sphere, in the eye of God. So embracing it all around—a fathomless heaven at every angle and aspect—sweeps the firmament of his love, on which eternal principles glow with steady flame, holding to rhythm and harmony the constellated truths which wheel around and among them. It doubtless seems to every soul that it sits in the centre of all this great system of things—that God is directly above it—that the essential truths which have relation to life are those, and only those, that come within the range of its vision; and it wonders how other souls can possibly live and thrive while looking out upon God and the firmament of love and truth from other points of vision. Yet, as a matter of fact, all Christian men see the same sun, and the same heaven of truth—only they see them from different angles.

I am aware that the two subjects which I have associated together in this article only touch each other at certain points; but those are important ones, and justify that which might otherwise appear far-fetched and arbitrary. My aim has simply been to arouse the mind of the reader to a more just and impartial estimate of those acts denominated sins, and to refer the minds of those who are inclined to sit in judgment upon their fellows, to the legitimate standard of judgment. A man does not necessarily sin who does that which our reason and our conscience condemn. A man is not necessarily in error who entertains views and opinions widely different from ours. We are constantly prone to fix arbitrary values upon our own good deeds, and to exaggerate evils that we see in other systems of belief, and sins that we see in other men. The true Christian charity is doubtless that which grows out of true Christian love. Essential Christian brotherhood is doubtless based in the common possession and entertainment of the divine life, though that life exist amid error and sin and ignorance, through the wide range of differing beliefs. But if we cannot have these realized as we would have them, we can have something which counterfeits them, and is better, on the whole, than nothing. We can have a charity growing out of a common consciousness of weakness, shortsightedness and sin, and a brotherhood of common imperfection.

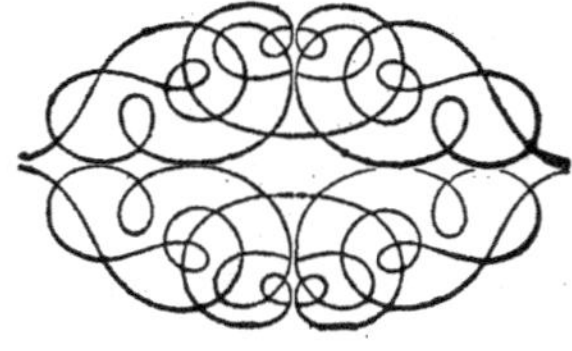

XVII.

THE CANONIZATION OF THE VICIOUS.

"Carrion crows bewail the dead sheep, and then eat them."

"'Ladies have ladies' whims,' said Crazy Ann, when she draggled her cloak in the gutter."

"The dog gets into the mill under cover of the ass."

"He that spares vice wrongs virtue."

AS there is one class of men in the world which is interested in magnifying the sins of others, so there is another, hardly less numerous, bent upon making the sins of others respectable. Out of this disposition and policy spring many of the celebrations of the birth-days of men whose lives have successfully associated splendid genius with ungovernable passions, great intellectual achievements with detestable vices, and admirable works with weak or wicked lives. So far has this been carried, that there exists, more or less definite, in the public mind, the impression that great genius and low morals are generally found together, and that, in some way, the former justifies, and, in some instances, even glorifies, the latter. A drunken physician is supposed to be very much better than any other physician, "if you can only catch him when he is sober," and it is imagined that there is somewhere a mysterious but very fruitful connection between the disposition to sottishness and skill in the treatment of disease.

I believe it is universally conceded that "the Man Christ Jesus" lived a purer life than any other man, sympathized with the poor and the lowly as no other man ever sympathized, did more for the comfort and the elevation of the humble and the wretched than any other, impressed himself upon the civilization of the world beyond all predecessors and successors, and revealed a religion which, over-arching all the elaborations of human philosophy, imparts to them whatever of significance they possess, and holds in itself alone the power of regenerating humanity; but, outside of the church, there are none who, of their own motion, meet to celebrate his birth-day. I have never heard of the celebration of the birth-day of John Milton, the great bard who sat in darkness, and evolved his more than mortal dreams, and who, grappling with immortal themes, wrested from them immortality for himself and the language in which he wrote. I see no tributes paid by the world to the memory of Montgomery. I never had the opportunity of drinking a toast to the gentle Christian, Cowper, or filling a bumper to Isaac Watts, whose lyric muse has given wings to more hearts burdened with praise and surcharged with aspiration than that of any other man since the sweet singer of Israel. I have never had an invitation to a dinner given to the memory of Howard, whose life was one of Humanity's most touching poems; or attended a supper in honor of Martin Luther. I find the great of the world—who were good in their greatness and great in their goodness—pretty generally let alone by the men who are accustomed to express their obligations to those who have been pre-eminent in government, literature, and art, while the memory of men whose weaknesses called for an extra cloak of pity, and whose vices made sight drafts on all the ready charity in the market, were toasted to the echo.

No great man who has scandalized his age by his personal vices, or done violence to the avowed principles of his public life by a great apostasy, can fall without drawing to his funeral all the apostates around him —men clinging to him by the sympathy of vice and falsehood, and using that sympathy as a platform which shall elevate them into the respectability which his genius won for him. Even the manes of Tom Paine is annually summoned into the congenial atmosphere of the banquet-hall, to make respectable by its power and fire an infidelity and libertinism which stink in the nostrils of a Christian nation, and which otherwise would suffocate themselves in their own effluvia.

Everybody knows how it is with the memory of Burns. It cannot well be doubted that more revellers assemble every year to celebrate his memory, through sympathy with the steaming whiskey which he loved so well, than with the aroma of his genius. "Poor Burns!" they exclaim; "what a pity he drank!" "Gifted Burns! Child of Nature! Let us forgive him that his gifts were not dedicated to the promotion of the purity which hallows the names of mother, sister, and wife!" "Sad dog, that Burns! True, he loved wine and women; but then, didn't he suffer for it? Let us compassionate him. He wasn't so much to blame, after all. The only wonder is how a man, with the tremendous fire-works he had in him, did not blow up with the first flash of a woman's eyes that smote him." And thus, the carrion crows bewail the dead sheep, and then eat them. Thus, with cloaks covered with the mud of the gutter, they flock together to contemplate the mud that a prostituted genius has gathered upon its garments, and foster their self-complacency by charitably transmuting its sins into whims. Thus the dogs endeavor to get into the mill under cover of the ass.

One of the most mischievous and fallacious of the current notions of an easily-erring world I conceive to be that which makes the possession of great gifts, and the achievement of great works, an offset to, or an apology for, indulgence in vices which compromise individual and social purity, and outbreaks of passion that come within the cognizance of the police. I believe that I respect all there is to be respected in the memory of Burns; but he was a weak—in many respects a vicious—and, in most respects, a miserable—man. He was the slave of a debasing appetite, and though, at brief intervals, he surrendered himself to the higher and purer inspirations that floated down to him from heaven, he loved to put them aside, and envelop himself in an atmosphere of sensuality. If he had a manly sense of manhood, wakened into life by the arrogance of wealth and place, it found its issue in words and not in life. It was the outburst of a protesting impulse rather than the self-assertion of a principle standing in the centre of the motive forces of his being.

Burns has left enough upon record to show that he possessed the subtlest apprehension of all that is noble in religion, all that is sweet and pure in woman, all that is strong and fruitful in manly virtue, and all that is praiseworthy in individual and national character. His best poem, "The Cotter's Saturday Night," is a revelation, clear as light, of his knowledge of goodness, and his convictions touching that which is noblest and truest in life. By a kind of necessity he, and all the brotherhood of vice-enslaved genius, have been made to reveal such a degree of knowledge of the truest truth and the best goodness, that all apology for their inconsistent and inconstant lives must be gratuitous. If great men have great passions, they have great minds with which to regulate and keep them in subjection; and in the degree in which God has given them power to move the hearts and attract the admiration of men, are they bound to teach, by word and pen, and exemplify by life, that which is truest and best in their convictions, and divinest in their faculties.

There is an abundance of vice in the world that legitimately calls for our charity, but it is not that which is associated with such genius as fully apprehends the beauty and the claims of virtue. Goethe is one of the great—Goethe, "the many sided man," Goethe, the man of science, the poet, the philosopher—yet his life was almost an unmitigated nuisance. If he ever failed to be a curse to a woman with whom he was thrown into association, it was not because he failed in effort for that end. The beast that was in him toyed through more than a filthy half century with the most delicate instincts and the most sacred sympathies of the female nature. Yet there are those who beg us not to judge Goethe too harshly—who bid us remember the power of his passions and the license of the age in which he lived. It is a competent answer to this plea to say that Goethe was as cool a man—a man as thoroughly under self-control—as any whose history we know; and that he flagrantly scandalized even the age which is thrust forward as his apology. I say, that to treat such a life as his with any thing softer than downright execration—to drape it with the velvet of charity, and trim it with silky apologies, is an outrage—direct and indefensible—upon the cause of virtue in the world.

While vice is made venial when associated with transcendent powers; while tributes of honor are offered to the memory of lives perverted, by men who have a covert interest in making perverted lives respectable; while even good men allow their admiration of genius to soften their judgments upon its prostitution, and substitute for a well-earned condemnation, a magnanimous gratuity of pity, it will not be strange if men with smaller intellects find excuse for such license of appetite and passion as they may see fit to indulge in.

Our literary Pet got drunk, and sung about it, in a rollicking way, and we weep and smile as we think of the debauchee, and say, "Poor Pet!" Tom Jones gets drunk, and we kick him as he lies in the gutter, refuse to recognize him when he gets upon his feet, and blame the police if he fail to get into the watch-house. Our Pet, armed with the enginery of a smooth tongue, well practiced in all the arts of intrigue and deception, besieges the citadel of a woman's heart, and, standing once within it, sets it on fire, and lays it in ashes. We sigh, and say, "Sad Pet!" Tom Jones betrays the confidence of his neighbor's daughter, in imitation of Our Pet's example, and gets his brains blown out, and we say it served him right. Our Pet was improvident. He spent his money without a thought of the debts he owed, or the cash he had bor rowed; and we say, "Unfortunate Pet! He did not seem to know any thing of the value of money!" Tom Jones borrows money, runs in debt, and forgets to pay; and we conclude that the rascal has no very acute sense of moral obligation—in fact, that Tom Jones is a swindler. Now, I have an idea that a moral code that is good enough for Our Pet is good enough for Tom Jones, and that Tom Jones has good cause of complaint when treated more harshly by the decent public than his great exemplar.

I cannot help thinking that the indulgence with which great men are treated by the world, in their moral obliquities and eccentricities, has much to do in making them what they are. An unprincipled man of genius who can achieve and maintain power over the minds of good men, independently of his moral character, and secure at the same time the sympathy and support of bad men, by participating in their vices, will always do both. The prevalent disposition which I see on all sides to make heroes and martyrs of the infamous great, amounts to a premium on all that is despicable and horrible in unbridled ambition and limitless lust. What means the attempt of the world's greatest living writer to apotheosize the brute whose choice it was to be buried with his horse? What will its effect be but to obliterate moral distinctions, and lift up for imitation a character as much out of place in this Christian age as a wild boar would be in a conference meeting?

Within the last three years, hundreds of thousands of hearts have been turned in sympathy and affection toward the character and life of one who sacrificed upon the altar of his rabid ambition hecatombs of his countrymen, and filled all Europe with the wails and curses of widows and orphans,—of one who had no God higher than Fate, acknowledged no leader but Destiny, and who, in following her, put to shame all of manhood in mankind by trampling under his feet a true heart and a sacred vow, that the Devil might give him the child that God had denied to him. What will the effect of this be upon ambitious natures, but to prove that a man has only to use all of the world he can lay his hands on for selfish ends, to secure the services of a Christian eulogist? Even Aaron Burr, the infamous traitor, murderer, and libertine, finds a man to speak well of him—praise only assuming the significance of a harmless joke, in consequence of the freshness of the stench which his memory has left behind him.

Over all that realm, where high or humble mind is struggling honestly with the great problems that concern its spiritual life and its immortal destiny—struggling toward the light through devious ways of error—I would see a broad-winged liberality spread its luminous shadow. To all those whose education in the truth has been limited, whose circumstances of life have been adverse to the development of purity, who are weak and ignorant, and low in instinct and aspiration, I would extend a charity that pities while it blames, and considers while it condemns. But to sin in high places—among men and women who are crowned kings and queens in the realm of intellect—those whose brows have been lifted into God's own light, and whose tongues and pens reveal something of the divinity which struggles to enthrone itself in them—no excuses, no palliations, no patronage. Over a great, bad life, let us sigh once, and then be silent; and when we choose among the memories of memorable men for the subject of a public tribute or a personal eulogy, let us take one out of which shall spring inspirations to a pure life, and motives to a noble heroism. When we choose heroes for deification, let them at least believe in the God who made them, and present a life for delineation and contemplation unblotched by all the sins forbidden by the Decalogue.

He who spares vice or apologizes for it in the high

places of the world, wrongs virtue in every place. He helps the good to look upon it leniently, and thus to lower the tone of morality within themselves. He assists the bad to make it respectable, and thus to give them warrant and license in its imitation, and even in its emulation. He discourages virtue in the humble and poor—the great masses who form the real basis of society, and upon whose goodness and truth the state must rely for its character before the world, and its stability in the world. He disturbs the moral apprehensions and unsettles the moral balance of all to whom his words and influence come. Let us braid no more wreaths to hide the mark of Cain on the brow of murder. Let us send up no more clouds of incense to veil the front of shame. The intellect will bow, if it must, but let it be with a protesting tongue and arms closely folded over the heart!

XVIII.

SOCIAL CLASSIFICATION.

"When the crane attempts to dance with the horse, she gets broken bones."

"Like plays best with like."

"It is dangerous to eat cherries with the great; they throw the stones at your head."

"Like seeks like—a scabbed horse and a sandy dike."

THERE is a very general entertainment of the fallacy that all the distinctions of society are artificial. I call it a fallacy, because I believe it to be susceptible of proof that the most of them are natural. The aristocracy of a town or state is always founded upon what the majority of the people of such town or state hold to be the chief good. No class arrogates to itself the aristocratic position without the accordance, tacit or declared, of all classes. Wherever noble family descent is popularly regarded as the most honorable of all things, aristocracy is founded upon blood. Wherever high intellectual culture is accounted the most honorable of all possessions, the aristocracy will be composed of savans, poets, artists, and men and women of brilliant parts and attainments. So, too, where money is regarded universally as the chief good, alike by rich and poor, the aristocratic element will reside in wealth. It would be easy to cite specimens of these varieties of aristocracy. I suppose that Paris, as the representative of France, furnishes an instance of the aristocracy of talent and culture; that London represents England in its aristocracy of blood, and that New York represents America in the aristocracy of wealth. In each of these types there is a blending of the other two. The three herd together, more or less, but the nucleus is distinct in each, and the other elements crystallize around it.

So I say that the aristocracy of any country is nothing more than a declaration, in conventional form, of that country's sentiment and opinion upon the chief earthly end of man. Every aristocrat is made such by a popular vote; and by the same vote is he endowed with all the privileges, immunities, pride, superciliousness, and exclusiveness which are supposed to pertain to the aristocratic estate. It matters nothing how humble, genial, and good a popularly constituted aristocrat may be, he gets little credit for it, for the people regard him as a superior, who can only be humble by condescension, genial for a purpose, and good by anomalous exception. Having entered the charmed circle of those who have won the highest prize of life, his old friends forsake him, misconstrue him, and force him into aristocratic association, whether he will or no. There is no aristocratic class in any state possessing institutions measurably free, which can sustain itself for ten years beyond the choice and voice of the people.

I have no idea that while human society exists there will fail to exist an aristocratic element, for so long as human society exists there will exist a popular ideal of a chief good, the achievement of that good by a fortunate few, and the association of that fortunate few, by natural affinity and corresponding position. If this class exist, other classes will exist, receding, by grades more or less distinctly defined, to the lowest figure of the scale—all measurably regulated by this idea of the chief good and the degree of its attainment; measurably, I say, for there are subordinate standards of respectability, as well as affinities of natural temperament and business pursuit, that come in as modifying influences. So I say that classes exist in society by a law as immutable as any law. They always have existed, and they always will—their character determined by the character and aims of the people, and their relations regulated by the spirit of the people.

On this track of general statement I proceed to the lesson of this article. The more readily to arrive at this lesson, let us institute an experiment. Let us bring together, to form a single social assembly, representatives from each of the classes that we know, and see how they will get along together. Let us shut into a single parlor a Marquis, a savan, a Crœsus, a farmer, a merchant, a tallow-chandler, a blacksmith, an Irish hod-carrier, a stage-driver, a dancing-master, a fop, a fool, and a fiddler. They come together for social enjoyment; and the question as to how much of that article they will be able to obtain is that to which I ask an answer. All the probabilities are against any thing like enjoyment. There are no tastes accordant, no pursuits common, no habits of thought at all similar, no common ground of communion. I can imagine no other position in which any member of the company could be placed where he would be more utterly miserable. The hod-carrier would probably feel the worst of the whole number, and would wish himself a thousand times on the topmost round of a seven-story ladder, while only the fool would be the subject of envy.

We should have, in an experiment like this, the demonstration of the truth of one of our proverbs, that "like plays best with like." There is not, and there can never be, social enjoyment without social sympathy. In all healthfully organized social life there must be correspondence of position, of education, of moral sentiment, and of habits of thought and life—a correspondence with limits of variation which every class tacitly acknowledges. This sympathy is born of facts, and not of will. A man sees a circle with which he has had no association; and, as he deems its entrance desirable, he accomplishes his desire, only to find himself a discordant element, and, consequently, an unhappy one. In short, there is a class with wh.ch each man has more sympathy than with any other class,—a class in which he finds himself the happiest and the most at home. Therefore he belongs in this class, socially; and he will go above it, if there be any thing above it, and below it, if there be any thing below it, only to make himself, and those with whom he associates, uncomfortable.

I have frequently noticed the operation of this law in a large circle of women met to prosecute an object of benevolence, as in the sewing circles connected with the various religious organizations. They meet for a common object. They all have respect for each other, and a pleasant word for each other. There are no jealousies and no rivalries. They pass their afternoon and evening happily, and separate with mutual good feeling; yet one who knows them all sees the secret of their concord, in the way in which they associate.

Never, unless a directly opposing design, instituted for a purpose, interfere, do they mingle indiscriminately The rooms where they meet, and even the corners of the rooms, are so many nuclei of crystallization, around which sympathetic social elements arrange themselves for communion and happiness. They follow the general law inside of their organization, just as naturally as they do out of it. Like talks best with like, laughs best with like, works best with like, and enjoys best with like; and it cannot help it. Therefore, let like come together with like everywhere, nor seek to prevent it, for social position, under the general law, elevates no one and depresses no one. It is simply a classification of individualities, according to conditions and sympathies which exist independent of class, and which would exist all the same were they not brought into association.

I have thus exhibited what I believe to be the rational basis of social classification—a law as certain in its operation as the law of chemical affinity, and one which I believe to be founded in unmixed benevolence. I have done it for the purpose of exhibiting the unreasonableness and the mischief of jealousy between classes, and especially that entertained by classes nominally low in the social scale toward those nominally high. A man in the lower class may be as good as a man in the higher. He may, in fact, be much better;

but so long as he combines with others in making the chief earthly good to reside in wealth rather than wisdom, in gold rather than goodness, he must not complain if those who get wealth get superior position, while wisdom and goodness are at a discount. The spirit and aim of a nation inevitably fix the basis of its aristocracy. This nation is mad for gold, and those who get it will inevitably be the central and controlling element in the nation's highest social class. There is no way under heaven to change this fact but by changing the popular aim. Make high culture or great excellence of character the leading aim of the country, and then you will get your chance. All that goodness and wisdom enjoy of social eminence, save in special localities, is through the patronage of wealth. This I state as the general fact with relation to this country. In other countries, where the leading aristocratic element resides in nobility, or intellectual pre-eminence, these respectively become the patrons of the elements thrown into inferior relation.

Every man is a common centre of multiplied circles of association. First in order is the family circle; embracing that is the circle of remoter kindred; beyond that, at longer or shorter distances, sweeps around the social circle. Then comes the circle of religious fraternity; then the political circle; then the broad circle of human brotherhood, embracing family, kindred, society, the church, the state, and the world; and still more broadly sweeping, runs the golden chain that encloses each soul in the universe within the sphere of relation to all created intelligences. These are all natural circles—or circles dependent on natural law for their definition. Family and kindred are based in natural affection, growing out of identity of blood. Society is based in natural affinity and similarity and sympathy of position and pursuit. The church is formed by sympathy of religious belief; the state by a common political creed and common institutions; and so on to the utmost boundary of relationship. From each minor circle all outside of it are shut out; yet, as the circles enlarge, all come upon a common level. In the state, we are fellow-citizens; in the church, we are Christian brethren. In all our higher and more majestic relations, the hands of mankind are joined. We sit at the same communion table, we bow to the same law and the same Lord, we cast an equal ballot.

Now, as to the matter of duty with relation to these social circles; no man should despise the circle n which he finds himself, but should seek to elevate and make it better. There are positions of power and usefulness in each circle, worthy of any man's ambition; while the entrance to another circle, nominally higher, under the patronage of its central, controlling element, is a disgrace to any man. A man willingly patronized, is a man voluntarily disgraced; and a man who seeks for respectability in a social position into which he does not naturally fall, shows himself to be lacking both in sense and self-respect.

Nothing but a popular change in the standard of respectability can ever make the first social classes in this country what they should be; and that change, sooner or later, will as surely come as the redemption of the world to the highest type of Christian manhood shall come. When manhood becomes the leading object of humanity, then the books of heraldry, and the diplomas of the schools, and the ledgers of wealth, will cease to furnish passports to respectability. Until that period shall arrive, wealth and blood and intellectual attainment, without the slightest reference to morality or religion, as standards of character and life, will hold the social sway of the world. And this is right. It is as God made it, and would have it. It is the result of the operation of one of his irreversible laws. It is the popular penalty of a popular sin. To hasten the arrival of that period, it should be the aim of every man, laboring faithfully and diligently where God has placed him, to elevate the standard of respectability to the place where God would have it. Whenever the great popular voice practically declares that Christian manhood is the chief good, Christian manhood will take its position at the head of the social life of this country, and of the world. Then, if a man be not admitted to it, it will simply be because he is not good enough; for like will come together with like, by a natural law.

I would not say that there is no Christian manhood in the aristocracy of this country. I believe there is—that there is as much there as anywhere. I simply say that Christian manhood and womanhood are not credentials which of themselves secure high social recognition. They achieve their position by circumstance, and not by character; for the successful stock-gambler and the libertine stand side by side with them, upon an equal footing. That this fact should not be, is very evident; that this fact is, is chargeable upon all classes alike; and they have no just cause of quarrel with it, so long as they manifest no disposition to change it, by instituting another standard.

XIX.

THE PRESERVATION OF CHARACTER.

"A full vessel must be carried carefully."

"He is so full of himself that he is quite empty."

"If you had had fewer friends and more enemies you had been a better man."

"That is often lost in an hour which costs a lifetime."

AN observing man is never without sources of amusement, and it is certain that among these sources the unconscious devices resorted to for the creation and preservation of character, in the eye of the world, deserve a prominent place. We meet in every town men who feel that they have filled up the measure of their character, and have nothing further to do in life but to bear that character, like a full vessel, to their graves, without spilling a drop. They walk the streets as if they were bearing it upon their heads. They bow to their acquaintances with the consciousness of their precious burden constantly uppermost. They refrain from all complication with the stirring questions of the times through fear of a fatal jostle. They speak guardedly, as if a word might jar their priceless vase from the poise of continence. There is nothing so important to them as what they are pleased to consider their character; consequently, that is al-always to be consulted before any course of action can be determined upon. All questions of morality and reform, all matters of public or political interest, all personal associations, are considered primarily with reference to this character. If they prove to be consistent with it, and seem calculated to reveal something more of its glory, they are entered upon, or adopted; otherwise, they are discarded.

When a man arrives at a point where the preservation of his character becomes the prime object of his life, he may be considered a harmless man, but one upon whom no further dependence can be placed in carrying on the work of the world. As a member of society, he becomes strictly ornamental. We point to him as one of the ripe fruits of our civilization. We bring him out on great occasions, and show him. We make him president of conventions and benevolent associations. We introduce strangers to him that they may be impressed. We chronicle his arrival at the hotels. We burn incense before him, because we know it will please him, and because we know that he rather expects it. Small children regard him in respectful silence as he passes. He becomes one of our institutions, like a City Hall or an old church. We always know where to find him, as we do a well-established town-line. But one thing we never do; we never go to him in an emergency that demands risk and self-sacrifice, because we know that those things are not in his line. His character is the first thing, and that is to be taken care of. When we want any thing of this kind done, we go to men who have no character, or, having one, are not uncomfortably conscious of it.

Good and harmless as these people usually are, sources as they are of amusement to those who understand the secret springs of their life, fine as they are when regarded as specimens, they are, nevertheless, the victims of a mistake. Personal character with them has come to be the grand object of life—personal character as a thing of popular repute, when it should always be a resultant of true action, instituted for unselfish purposes. The meanest and the most illegitimate of all human pursuits, is the direct pursuit of a reputation. It is supremely selfish and contemptible; and there is no man who really deserves a good reputation who does not make its acquisition subordinate, as an aim, in all his actions. A man whose action with relation to the questions that come before him is regulated by its preconceived effect upon his character with the public, is entirely untrustworthy, and will be trusted by the public no further than his interest is seen to coincide with the wishes of the public.

Character is a thing that will take care of itself; and all character that does not take care of itself is either very weak, or utterly fictitious. A man who does as nearly right as possible, according to the dictates of his judgment and his conscience, will achieve a character without giving a thought to it, so that all attention bestowed upon the direct acquisition of character before the public, is so much attention wasted and so much time thrown away. By their works are we to know men; and we have no other standard by which to measure them. We tolerate a harmless, selfish man, but we do not trust him with our interests. The most of those whom we find supremely devoted to the preservation of their character, won their character honestly enough, originally. They struck out boldly at the beginning of life, did nobly, succeeded, won the praise of the people, and then, like men grown rich, became suddenly conservative and timid. Finding themselves in possession of a character, and realizing something of the preciousness of the possession, they immediately began to nurse it, and arrange all their action with relation to it. Then they ceased to grow, and retired essentially from business.

Much better would it have been for all of this class had they had fewer friends and more enemies. In fact, there is a fault in the reputation of every man who has no enemies, for no man can be a positive power in the world, moving in right lines through evils, and abuses, and wrongs, without treading upon the toes of somebody. As this world is constituted, no man can be without enemies unless he be without power, or unless he adapt himself to the evils and the evil men encountered in his course. Consequently, no man has a reputation which is really significant and valuable that is not won in about equal measure from the blessings of one class and the curses of another. The praises of the good are no better testimonials of a sound and valuable character than the maledictions of the bad. In fact, reputation and character are widely different things, though they are so closely coupled in the minds of those whom we are discussing that they see no difference between them. Character lives in a man; reputation outside of him. A man may have a good character and no reputation, or he may have a good reputation and no character; but with self worshippers they are nearly identical.

Of all the bondage in the world I know of none more senseless and useless than bondage to one's character or reputation. The "fogyism" and "hunkerism" of politics, and the rigid conservatism of religious opinion, grow mainly out of this bondage. Consistency is clung to with almost an insane tenacity. It is more important in this bondage that a course of action should be consistent with a man's past life than with truth and justice. A man's past is elevated as the highest standard of his present and his future. He pledges himself against progress by making his present character and his past course the law of his life. He clings to the institutions, the opinions, the policy, and the sentiments in which he has cast his life; and when these are gone, or are superseded, he clings to their names, and so "walks in vain show." If a party dies, it does not die to him; because, if he were to admit the fact, or the idea, of its death, he would doubt his own infallibility. If an institution falls, he will not acknowledge it, for it will make a hole in a reputation which he considers compacted and complete. No man who progresses can be consistent with himself. Maturity cannot be consistent with immaturity. All the consistency God requires of any man, or approves in any man, is consistency with the best light of the present. Let the dead bury its dead. It is only God himself who has even the right to be consistent with His past life.

The worthy young men who read these words are dreaming of the attainment of a character which shall give them not only reputation—not only praise—but weight in the world. If this be your prime object, young man, you are very likely to take the wrong course and make wreck of yourself. Let me tell you that if you do right, your character will take care of itself, no less than your reputation. Serve God and your generation well, leave the consideration of your character and yourself behind, seek to be consistent with the highest life you have, be not afraid to change your opinions or your course on any thing if you think you are wrong, and God and your generation will take care of you. As soon as it is seen that you are unselfish, and that you are free to act rightly and justly with relation to whatever comes before you, a place in the world will be made for you, and work will be given you to do. Do not be disheartened if you make enemies, for if you are really a good power in the world, you will be sure to make them. I do not say that a man who has enemies is necessarily a good man, but I do say that no man can be a good power in the world without making them.

There are a hundred things that I could mention more valuable than reputation. Self-respect is one of these; a conscience void of offence is another; the reformation and the progress of those around you are others; and God's approval is another. Maintain your self-respect; keep a spotless conscience; and do good to all around you with supreme reference to Him in whom you live, and your character will grow healthfully, without a thought given to it. The moment the preservation of your character and reputation becomes the great object of your life,—the moment that you begin to arrange your life with reference to a character already achieved—that moment you will cease to grow, and pass to your place among the harmless fossils that occupy the ornamental niches of society.

The influence of enemies upon a really sound character is always healthful. A certain degree of recognition and praise does any man good; but the usual effect of a great deal of it is debilitating. It spoils the child, and weakens the preacher, and enervates the orator. It injures the character of almost every man. Praise is very sweet, but the soul cannot thrive upon a diet of sugar any more than the body. A man who receives a great deal of praise, and drinks it in with genuine appetite, soon comes to regard it with an unhealthy greed. He wants it from every body, wants it all the time, labors to get it, and is disappointed and uneasy if he does not get it. It is well for every man, therefore, to have enemies, to hear what they say about him, and to experience the weight of their opposition. Enemies drive the soul home to its motives, rouse its finest energies, compact its character, render it watchful of the issues of its life, keep it strained up to its work, and help to eliminate from it selfish considerations. There hardly ever lived a reformer who might not have been strangled and silenced at the outset of his career by praise. Thank God for the enmity that developed into giants the reformers of our own and of past times. May He in mercy forbid that any of the young and noble hearts now yearning for the good work of the world be spoiled by too much praise and too few enemies!

A character once worthily won is to be preserved in precisely the same way that it is won. A character is easily tarnished, and a good name easily lost; but neither is to be preserved by making it the supreme object of attention. Here it becomes necessary to keep a broad distinction between reputation and character, for one may be destroyed by slander, while the other can never be harmed save by its possessor. The malice of others may tarnish a good name—may load it with suspicions—may associate it with gross scandal—may blacken it even beyond the reach of total recovery, but the character can receive no injury save by the voluntary act and choice of its owner. A man, in order to retain his reputation, may be required, not unfrequently, to compromise his character; and in order to keep his character pure, may be obliged to compromise his reputation. Character is as much more valuable than reputation, as it is more valuable than its own name.

Reputation is in no man's keeping. You and I cannot determine what other men shall think of us and say about us. We can only determine what they ought to think of us and say about us; and we can only do this by acting squarely up to our convictions of duty, without the slightest reference to its effect upon ourselves. There are two ways in which men lose their character and their reputation with it. The selfish means instituted for the direct purpose of preserving character and reputation are damaging to any man. How many statesmen and politicians have "fixed themselves up" with a character which every one sees is intended for a market, and how few of all the number ever arrive at the goal of their ambition! Many of them become the laughing-stock of the country; and when the great conventions meet, their names are passed by, and new ones elevated, of those who have been employed in minding their business, and letting their character and reputation take care of themselves. One great reason why so few of the truly great men of the nation have failed to be placed in the presidential office is that they spoiled their reputation in the selfish desire to preserve it for the purpose of winning office.

Another way of losing character and reputation is by yielding to some sudden temptation to sin, or by the secret entertainment of a vice that with certainty undermines both. A single deed of shame, ah! how it blackens beyond all cleansing the character that has been builded in the struggles and toils of half a century! There is no wealth under the sun so precious as a good name worthily won, and there is no calamity so great as such a name shamefully lost. Far be it from me to depreciate the value of character, or to depreciate pride in its maintenance. While it should be the natural, unsought consequent of a life controlled by the purest and noblest motives, it doubtless may be entertained as a choice possession, always subordinate as a motive of action to Christian principle and duty.

XX.

VICES OF IMAGINATION.

'It is dangerous playing with edged tools."
"He who avoids the temptation avoids the sin."
"Keep yourself from opportunities, and God will keep you from sins."
"The pitcher that goes often to the well gets broken at last."

THERE is an enchanted middle ground between virtue and vice, where many a soul lives and feeds in secret, and takes its payment for the restraint and mortification of its outward life. I once knew an old dog whose most exalted and delighted life was lived upon this charmed territory. The only brute tenants of the dwelling where he lived were himself and a cat. Rover bore no ill-will toward his feline companion—in fact, he was too good-natured to bear ill-will toward any thing. He had been detected once or twice in worrying her, and one or two severe floggings had taught him that the sport would not be tolerated. Still he did not stop thinking about it; and at every convenient opportunity he planted himself in her way, watched her as she lurked for prey, scared her by growls and feints, and kept her in a fever of ap prehension and fretfulness. Now, while I do not be lieve that he intended her the slightest mischief, I have no doubt that, in his bloody imagination, he had slain her a thousand times, chased her all over the neighborhood, and torn her limb from limb. In short, while he knew that he must not worry her, he took the satisfaction that lay next to it—that of being tempted to worry her, and found in the excitements of this temptation the highest rewards of his self-denial.

Humanity has plenty of Rovers of this same sort—men and women who lead faultless outward lives, who have no intention to sin, who yield their judgment—if not their conscience—to the motives of self-restraint but who, in secret, resort to the fields of temptation, and seek among its excitements for the flavor, at least, of the sins which they have discarded. This realm of temptation is, to a multitude of minds, one of the most seductive in which their feet ever wander. Thither they resort to meet and commune with the images, beautiful but impure, of the forbidden things that lie beyond. In fact, I have sometimes thought there were men and women who were really more in love with temptation than with sin—who, by genuine experience, had learned that feasts of the imagination were sweeter than feasts of sense. Whether this be the case or not. I have no doubt that the love of temptation, for the excitement which it brings, is very general, even with those whom we esteem as patterns of virtue. The surrender of the soul to these excitements is the more dangerous from the fact that, by some sort of sensual sophistry, they are conceived to be harmless, and without the pale of actual sin. There is no intention to sin in it, but only an attempt to filch from sin all the pleasure that can be procured without its penalty.

Playing with the temptation to sin is doubtless accompanied with less apparent disaster than the actual commission of it, and, so far, is a smaller evil; but it is an evil, and, essentially, a sin. The man who loves and seeks the excitement of temptation, shows that he is restrained from sin by fear, and not by principle—that, while his life is on the side of virtue, his affections lean to vice. This is a sham life, and a mean life. There are multitudes to whom temptation comes from the forbidden world of sin, but it comes unbidden an. unwelcome—on the lines of old appetites and old passions not yet thoroughly under control—and it is fought against and driven out. It is the voluntary going out of the soul after temptation, as a kind of unforbidden good, that I challenge and question. It is the willing, secret sin of imagination that I denounce, as not only a sin essentially, in itself, but as the path over which every soul naturally travels to the overt act of transgression which lies beyond. It is a kind of sin that injures none but the sinner, directly; but fouler, more rotten-hearted men I have never met than the cowardly hypocrites whose lives are spent in dallying with the thought of sins which they dare not commit.

We often wonder that certain men and women are left by God to the commission of sins which shock us. We wonder how, under the temptation of a single hour, they fall from the very heights of virtue and of honor into sin and shame. The fact is that there are no such falls as these, or there are next to none. These men and women are those who have dallied with temptation—have exposed themselves to the influence of it, and have been weakened and corrupted by it. If we could get at the secret histories of those who stand suddenly discovered as vicious, we should find that they had been through this most polluting preparatory process—that they had been in the habit of going out and meeting temptation in order that they might enjoy its excitements—that underneath a blameless outward life they have welcomed and entertained sin in their imaginations, until their moral sense was blunted, and they were ready for the deed of which they thought they were incapable.

I very earnestly and gratefully believe in the exercise of a divinely restraining influence upon the minds of those who are tempted, but I believe there is a point beyond which it rarely goes. I do not believe that God will interpose to prevent a man from sinning who either seeks, or willingly encounters, the temptation and the opportunity to sin. When a man finds charm in opportunity, and delight in temptation, he has already committed in heart the sin which he shrinks from embodying in action; and God rarely stands between him and further guilt. We are to keep ourselves from opportunities, and God will keep us from sin. It is all that can be expected of a being of infinite purity that he shall guard us from the power of temptation that comes to us. He must be a hard and irreverent, or a very ignorant and deluded man, who can pray to be delivered from the overcoming power of a temptation into whose atmosphere he willingly enters. In fact, we are taught to pray, not that we may be delivered from the power of temptation, but that we may not be led into it.

It may be said with measurable truthfulness that half the art of Christian living consists in shunning temptation. A man who has lived to middle life has observed and studied himself to little purpose if he have not learned the weak points of his own character, and the kind of temptations that assail him with the most power; and it is doubtless true that any man who really loves a pure and good life will avoid a temptation as he would the sin to which it would lead him. I can have but little charity for those who apologize for their frequent falls from virtue by charging the blame upon the power of temptation, because temptation and opportunity come to them unsought no oftener than to others. It is the man who loves vice, and delights in temptation, who is subject to their power. I have no faith in the reformation of a drunkard who carelessly passes his accustomed tippling-shop, and carelessly looks in.

We are to avoid temptation because it is only as vice is glorified, and its charms exalted by the power of imagination, that it appears charming and attractive to us. A vision of naked vice, of whatsoever sort, is a vision of deformity. There are thousands among those who delight in the excitements of temptation, voluntarily sought, who would shrink with horror and disgust from a sudden introduction to the presence of a vice toward which they have been attracted from a distance. There is no beauty in beastliness, save that which an excited imagination lends to it. It is by no inherent charm that it draws men and women toward it. It is as low and loathsome as the serpent around whose evil eyes the poor bird flutters, until it drops, a victim to the fangs that await its certain coming.

I have said thus much generally of the sins of the

imagination, aware that my remarks apply mainly to one variety of temptations—the most dangerous and the most seductive of all. There is nothing charming in the thought of murder, in the contemplation of a great revenge, in theft, and in the majority of crimes. Imagination has no sophistry by which such crimes may be justified, and no power to wrap them in an atmosphere of beauty. The sins of the imagination are mainly those which contemplate the illicit indulgence of natural and normal passions and appetites, the temptations to which come in upon the lines of legitimate and heaven-ordained sympathies. It is among the meshes of that which is legitimate and that which is illegitimate—that which is forbidden and that which is unforbidden—that the moral sense becomes involved and moral purity is compromised. It is because men and women are led out into the field of temptation by some of the sweetest and strongest sympathies of their natures that they feel no alarm and apprehend no danger. It is because they entertain no design to sin that they linger there without fear. Oh! if this imaginary world of sin could be unveiled—this world into which the multitude go unknown and unsuspected—to dream of delights unhallowed by relations that may only give them license—how would it be red with the blush of shame!

This world of sense, built by the imagination—how

fair and foul it is! Like a fairy island in the sea of life, it smiles in sunlight and sleeps in green, known of the world not by communion of knowledge, but by personal, secret discovery! The waves of every ocean kiss its feet. The airs of every clime play among its trees, and tire with the voluptuous music which they bear. Flowers bend idly to the fall of fountains, and beautiful forms are wreathing their white arms, and calling for companionship. Out toward this charmed island, by day and by night, a million shallops push unseen of each other, and of the world of real life left behind, for revelry and reward! The single sailors never meet each other; they tread the same paths unknown of each other; they come back, and no one knows, and no one asks where they have been. Again and again is the visit repeated, with no absolutely vicious intention, yet not without gathering the taint of vice. If God's light could shine upon this crowded sea, and discover the secrets of the island which it invests, what shameful retreats and encounters should we witness—fathers, mothers, maidens, men—children even, whom we had deemed as pure as snow—flying with guilty eyes and white lips to hide themselves from a great disgrace!

There is vice enough in the world of actual life, and it is there that we look for it; but there is more in that other world of imagination that we do not see—vice that poisons, vice that kills, vice that makes whited sepulchres of temples that are deemed pure, even by multitudes of their tenants. Let none esteem themselves blameless or pure who willingly and gladly seek in this world of imagination for excitements! That remarkable poem of Margaret Fuller, which ascribes an indelible taint to the maiden who only dreams of her lover an unmaidenly dream, has a fearful but entirely legitimate significance. It is a forbidden realm, where pure feet never wander; and all who would remain pure must forever avoid it. It is the haunt of devils and damned spirits. Its foul air poisons manhood and shrivels womanhood, even if it never be left behind in an advance to the overt sin which lies beyond it.

The pitcher that goes often to the well gets broken at last. I presume that there is not one licentious man or ruined woman in one hundred whose way to perdition did not lie directly through this forbidden field of imagination. Into that field they went, and went again, till, weakened by the poisonous atmosphere, and grown morbid in their love of sin, and developed in all their tendencies to sensuality, and familiarized with the thought of vice, they fell, with neither the disposition nor the power to rise again. It is in this field that Satan wins all his victories. It is here that he is transformed into an angel of light. It is on this debatable ground, half-way between vice and virtue, whither the silly multitude resort for dreams of that which they may not enjoy, that the question of personal perdition is settled. A pure soul sternly standing on the ground of virtue, or a pure soul standing immediately in the presence of vice, not once in ten thousand instances bends from its rectitude. It is only when it willingly becomes a wanderer among the wiles of temptation, and an entertainer of the images it finds there, that it becomes subject to the power that procures its ruin.

To the young, especially, is the exposition of this subject necessary—to those whose imaginations are active, whose passions are fresh and strong, and whose inexperience leaves them ignorant of consequences. There is no field of danger less talked of than this. Through many years of attendance upon the public ministrations of Christianity, I have never but twice heard this subject pointedly and faithfully alluded to. Books are mainly silent upon it. Fathers and mothers, faithful in all things else, shrink from the administration of counsels upon matters which they would fain believe are all unknown to the precious ones they have nurtured. Thus is it in schools, and thus is it everywhere, where counsel is needed, and where it is demanded. An impure word, a doubtful jest, a tale of sin, drunk in by these fresh souls, excites the imagination, and straightway they discover the field of contemplation, so full of danger and of death, and learn all its paths before they know any thing of the perils to which they subject themselves. Let me say to these, what they hear so little from other lips and pens, that whenever they find themselves attracted to it, they can never abide in it, or enter upon it, without taint and without sin. Sooner or later in their life will they find that from all willing dalliance with temptation, and unresisted entertainment of unworthy and impure imaginations, their character has suffered an injury which untold ages will fail to remedy.

XXI.

QUESTIONS ABOVE REASON.

"Anoint a villain, and he will prick you; prick a villain, and he will anoint you."

"Give a rogue an inch, and he will take an ell."

"He who lies down with dogs, gets up with fleas."

GOOD men never make any thing by treating villains as equals. A conscious villain who is treated as an equal by an honest man who is conscious of his villany, recognizes the man at once as a coward, and treats him accordingly. Treated as an inferior, a bad man becomes polite at once, or plays defiantly the bully and the blackguard that he is. We may go the world over without finding any man who, in his own soul, knows his place so well as a very bad man; and there is no way of securing his respect so easily as by giving him to understand that he is understood, and appreciated at his true value. Bow to him, and treat him like a gentleman, and he flounders and swaggers in the respectability conferred upon him. Shun him, or show him in any way that he is known and despised, and he becomes respectful and decent, nine times in ten. There is no social or Christian relation in which good and bad men are equals, and any good man who, for any cowardly reason, is willing to ignore the distinction, commits a crime against society and against Christianity, and secures to himself the contempt of those to whom he defers. Anoint a villain, and he will prick you; prick a villain, and he will anoint you.

I know of no whip so effectual in its power when held over the back of an unprincipled man as social proscription. The worst men, save in exceptional cases of brutal self-abandonment, have a longing for respectability. It is a hard thing for any man to walk through the streets, and meet among respectable men nought but stony faces, and to know that those faces are set simply against his sins. It is a hard thing for the worst men to feel that all good hearts and all decent hearths are shut against them, because their entrance would be regarded as a contamination. So these men strive to cheat us into respecting them by the assumption of false names, or endeavor to purchase respect and position by exhibitions of public spirit. The professional gambler, who is simply a leech upon the social body—who gets his living without earning it, and wins the wealth of others by games of chance—the most heartless, ruthless and mischievous of men—calls himself a sporting man, and loves to be called a sporting man. He would be much obliged to society if it would never mention the word "gambler" in connection with his name. In fact, he would be willing to sacrifice a little something for the public good, if by so doing he could keep his chin above water.

Again, give a rogue an inch, and he will take an ell. Any favor shown to such men as these is an essential license for further sin. They want countenance, and they seek it in many ways. If they can create a party for themselves, or manage to secure among men nominally respectable apologists and defenders, they are delighted, and feel themselves safer in their schemes and operations. We have only to recognize them as equals to lengthen the rope that holds them to decency. The moment I recognize a well known scoundrel as an equal, that moment I descend to his standard of morality or immorality, assist to lower the general standard of respectability, and furnish to him a new point of departure from which he may plunge into further scoundrelism. The fact is that no man who preys upon society for a livelihood, or habitually engages in practices which compromise social purity and good order, can, by possibility, be a gentleman; and no gentleman can deal with such a man on an equality, or eat of his dainties, or accept of his company or his favors, without compromising his position as a gentleman.

He who lies down with dogs gets up with fleas. When a decent man lowers his standard of respectability so far that he can consort with a foe to society and morality, he damages himself beyond cure, in most instances. Confounding moral distinctions and compromising with sin are dangerous operations. In the measure by which a decent man confers respectability upon a rascal, does the rascal transfer reproach to him. The act is one which changes both parties for the worse. A respectable man who comes to look with a degree of complacency upon one who has no title to respectability, is morally damaged. He becomes a weaker man, more open to temptation, and more liable to fall. The princely gamblers of New York and Washington understand this principle thoroughly, and initiate all their victims by bringing them into communion with rascality over their costly viands and their abundant wines and cigars. There is no common ground of communion between the two classes. There is not even debatable ground. The distinction is heaven-wide on its very face.

I have stated these facts, first, because they are true, and should be made useful; and, second, because they introduce me to, and assist to illustrate, a principle not sufficiently recognized in the contacts and contests of truth with falsehood in the moral and religious world. It will be remembered—for the occurrence was a recent one—that a champion of slavery and an opponent of slavery met in an American city as disputants or wranglers upon this question. If slavery were only a political question, a discussion like this might be legitimate, though it might not be very useful. But it is recognized everywhere as not only a political, but a moral question. I enter upon no discussion of this question, because it is not relevant to my present purpose, but I say that to the opponent of slavery the right of every man to life, liberty, and the pursuit of happiness, is a self-evident truth—a truth which calls not for argument but statement—a fundamental truth, which lies at the very basis of all freedom and all sound institutions. Now, the moment a man holding such a view as this meets a champion of slavery on even ground, to argue the question, he yields the battle, and is worsted before he opens his mouth. By consenting that the question admits of argument, for a moment, he yields ground which is impregnable, places himself on a common footing with his antagonist, and damages himself and his cause. I have seen Christian men enter into arguments with avowed infidels in bar-rooms and vicious assemblages, as a matter of duty; and such sights have always oppresssed me with a sense of humiliation. Infidelity is not the equal of faith in any sense. Light has no fellowship with darkness, and Christ no concord with Belial. Religion may enter a pothouse as a minister of good, but it may not lay aside its dignity to argue its rights and claims there. The moment that it does this, it is shorn of its power. A man in whom Christianity has become a life, knows that Christianity is a verity—knows that no argument under heaven can convince him of its falsehood. He knows that the highest claims of Christianity are not based in argument. He knows that he was not intellectually argued into religion, that he is not kept in it by force of argument or logic, and that the highest demonstration of the truth of Christianity which he possesses—his own individual experience—is precisely that which he cannot bring forward in any dispute with an infidel. The moment, therefore, that he comes down from the position of positive knowledge, and admits that there is room for argument, he surrenders the citadel, and the conflict is to be decided simply by personal prowess. The truth of Christianity admitted between two opponents, there is, of course, a legitimate theatre of discussion opened for questions connected with it; but until that be admitted, there can be no discussion that does not compromise the position and the power of him who enters as the champion of Christianity.

I say that infidelity is not the equal of faith, because, while infidelity abides in, and relies upon, pure reason, faith, with reason abundantly satisfied, relies upon the demonstrations of an experience which infidelity will reject as a matter of course. I say that faith and infidelity can never meet on common ground to argue the truth or falsehood of Christianity, because faith, as its first step, must surrender its stronghold, and yield the question to the arbitration of reason, by which it can never be settled. I say, further, that no Christian man has a right to do this, and that he cannot do it without weakening himself, and damaging his cause. I may be willing, and should be willing, to give my reasons for my belief in Christianity, but I should not be willing to surrender a question to the judgment of reason which I know and feel to be mainly out of its realm. There is nothing that infidelity more thoroughly delights in than argument, because, in argument, it brings faith down to its own level, and takes it at a disadvantage. It is lifted into importance and respectability by the consent of faith to meet it on common ground—ground where none but weak minds will ever meet it—minds that will be mastered in a battle of reason almost as a matter of course.

Many of the best things received into the belief and faith of the best men—things relating to the heart of the individual and the life of society—demand that they shall never be submitted to the combats and con clusions of reason on a common ground with error. A gentleman will not fight a duel with a churl, simply because the churl is not his equal. He could gain no victory that would compensate for the social disgrace involved in meeting an inferior on a footing of equality. Men of the world, who will scout my reasoning upon the management of a certain class of moral questions, will understand this illustration, and find it somewhat difficult, I imagine, to get away from it. It is recognized as a rule of law, based on a fundamental principle of justice, that a man shall be tried by his peers—a body of men capable of appreciating all the circumstances and evidence of his case, and dispossessed of those prejudices of class and condition which would have a tendency to mislead them. The same principle demands that all those questions, which relate to things above the realm of pure reason, shall be judged by those who are capable of appreciating, and willing to accept, the evidence that lies in that realm. As there is no confession of cowardice on the part of a gentleman who refuses to fight a churl, and no self-conviction of guilt in him who declines to be tried by other than his peers, so there is no admission of weakness on the part of him who refuses to place his faith on the footing of another man's infidelity, and to submit the questions touching his highest life, to the judgment of those who are incapable of understanding, and unwilling to admit, the evidence relating to them.

The power of Christianity before the world, as a system of religion, no less than the power of all those objects and subjects of faith and belief which lie above the domain of pure reason, abides in assertion—bold, broad, direct, confident, and persistent assertion. If a man were to deny that the rose is beautiful, and challenge me to the proof of its beauty, what more could I do than to hold the rose before his eyes, and say that it is beautiful? If the rose could speak, would it thank me for admitting that its beauty is a matter of argument? The settlement of the question of its beauty is utterly beyond the power of reason. I know it is beautiful; I feel that it is beautiful; its beauty thrills me with the most delicious pleasure. That is enough for me; but that would not be enough for him who denies its beauty. I arrive at a knowledge of its beauty by no process of reasoning, and I can maintain the fact of its beauty by no power of argument, because the determination of its quality and character is without the realm of reason.

In my judgment, a great mistake has been made by well-meaning and zealous men, through treating error and infidelity with altogether too much respect. I believe that it is safe to say that Christianity is indebted for none of its progress in the world to rational conflicts with infidelity. I do not believe that a single great wrong has ever been overthrown by meeting the advocates of wrong in argument. Assertion of truths known and felt, promulgation of truth from the high platform of truth itself, declaration of faith by the mouth of moral conviction—this is the New Testament method, and the true one. If a man say to me that he does not believe in the existence of a God, my judgment tells me at once that, if he is sincere, he is insane or a fool, and that if he is insincere, he is a liar. Shall I sit down to argue the question with him after this? Shall I admit that his atheism is as good as my belief? No. If he make his assertion, let him be content with that. If he ask of me the reason of my belief, I will give it him, but I will not admit that to be a subject of argument which is the first fact in the mental and moral universe. By so doing I should commit an absurdity that would stultify me, and inflict a dishonor on the Being of whom I make myself the champion.

If I have made myself understood on this point, I have dwelt upon it long enough, and have only to add, that he who allows himself to be placed in a false position by consenting to stand on the platform of reason, with relation to questions beyond the domain of reason, will find himself damaged in the end. If he lie down with dogs, he will get up with fleas. A man who consents to the purely rational decision of a question which reason can never settle, will find himself open to the invasions of error—weakened in all his defences. Forsaking an impregnable position, he enters a field full of doubts and dangers; and if he consent to remain there, he will become a subject of their attack at every point. More men have been argued, in a measure, or entirely, out of faith, than have ever been argued into it—not because their faith was irrational, but because they have prostituted that to the basis of reason which is beyond the realm of reason.

Assertion, proclamation, exhibition, illustration—these are the instruments of the progress of all truth relating to the highest life of the world. The Gospel is promulgated by preaching, not by wrangling. The reformation of the sixteenth century was effected by the assertion of a few simple truths, and the denunciation of errors and abuses. The idea of Luther consenting to meet Tetzel before a public audience, to argue the question of the legitimacy and morality of peddling indulgences to sin, is simply ridiculous. That thing was not to be soberly argued, but soundly denounced. No truth held to be self-evident, and no truth whose demonstration lies in personal experience—and therefore above reason—can ever be submitted to argument without prostitution or without danger. Reason dethroned truth in France, but truth resumed its seat, in spite of reason, by simple self-assertion. All truth that lives independent of reason asks no favors of it, and takes no law of it.

XXII.

PUBLIC AND PRIVATE LIFE.

"Many a cow stands in the meadow, and looks wistfully at the common."
"Grass grows not upon the highway."
"Life at court is often a short cut to hell."

THERE is no human estate or condition around which gathers so much that is fallacious in glory and fictitious in attraction as around that which is denominated "public life." To be exalted in public office, to be observed of a state or a nation, to be sought out and honored of public assemblages, to be known and recognized by the public press—this seems to a great multitude, whose fortunes are cast in private life, to be the most desirable, the most enviable thing, in all the world. If we could read the secret of nine hearts in ten that we meet, we should find that under their seeming content with private life and apparent satisfaction with private pursuits, there is a longing for a position that will give their persons, powers and names a public recognition. The greed for office, which is evident on every hand, and among all classes of people, is but a demonstration of this universal appetite. It is not confined to a sex, but manifests itself among women as well as among men. We hear much of "woman's rights," from the lips of women who have a taste for public life, or a desire for public recognition, and they make their proselytes among those who are exercised by a similar ambition.

It is a very sad thing to me—this discontent with private life—because the larger part of it has no noble element in it. The majority of men and women who are ambitious of public life do not wish for it for the sake of doing more good, nor because they believe themselves to be transcendently adapted to the performance of public duties. They are not willing to work and wait, in their private spheres of action, until they demonstrate their ability and fitness for public position, and are sought for by the public as those worthy of trust and honor. No, they desire place for the sake of place; they seek for public life simply from a greed for notoriety or fame. They desire to be known, to be looked at, to be talked about, to be lionized. It is publicity that has charms for them—not public duty, nor public responsibility. All this is utterly selfish—utterly contemptible. It is unworthy of sound manhood and true womanhood, and its tendency is directly demoralizing. When we remember that the public offices of the country are filled mainly by those who have attained them by direct seeking, spurred on by this base ambition, it will not be hard to account for the low morals that are to be found in public life.

We can go further than this. It may truthfully be said that a man whose chief ambition is publicity of name and position, demonstrates, by its possession and exercise, his unfitness for that to which he aspires. If in this great world of discontented private life there are men or women who read these words, let them consider that in the degree in which their ambition to be known is the predominant motive within them, do they demonstrate their unfitness for the honors which they seek. The ambition is essentially a selfish and a mean one, and proves directly, and unmistakably, the possession of a nature unworthy of great public responsibilities. A surpassing, overweening desire for public life, for the sake of public life, and the kind of honor which it brings, demonstrates a nature that will subordinate public to private good, and elevate personal reputation above the requirements of public duty. The cowardice of politicians, and the shameful devotion to private interests that prevails in legislative bodies, only show how many have found place through this selfish seeking of it.

But all public life, or all notoriety, is not to be found in politics. Literature, journalism, the pulpit, the bar—all these are aspired to as objects that are calculated, more or less, to satisfy the appetite for public notoriety. The consequence is that literature is crowded with weak or vicious pretenders, journalism with greedy self-seekers, the pulpit with men who have no qualifications for their calling, and the bar with brawling pettifoggers. The question with great numbers who embrace these professions is not—"What have I within me, for the world, that I may convey through the profession which I choose to the world?" but—"What has the world for me, that it can convey through this profession to me?" There is a proper kind of self-seeking, but it is that which has its basis in worthy doing. A man who gladly grasps an honor which he has not earned, because it is an honor, is a man unworthy of trust and without shame.

But is there any thing, after all, in this public life that is so very desirable? Is there any thing so very sweet in having one's name public property? Is there any thing in the burden of public responsibilities and cares that is so exceedingly pleasant to bear? I am willing that any man who bears worthily the burden of public life shall answer these questions. Any man who takes upon his shoulders, and faithfully and conscientiously carries, the responsibilities of a public position, knows and feels that he is a slave, and that the careless hind who whistles behind his plough has a peace of mind which has left him forever.

It matters not what kind of publicity or notoriety any man, worthy or unworthy, may have, he will be the object of the meanest envy and the most inveterate enmity. A name that has become public property is a name to be bandied about, coupled with foul epithets, criticised, contemned, or to be made the subject of extravagant laudation—more humiliating, if less maddening. The alternative of a public life of mingled praise and abuse, or of unmeasured abuse, is that of a public idol—is a public life that shall be the object of universal flattery. There are some men who can withstand the influences of such a position as this, but they are few, and far between. A public life is always a life of great temptation; and few lead it who do not feel, in the depths of their souls, that they have been damaged by it. A host of evil influences cluster about it. It interferes with domestic peace, absorbs the mind, and blunts the affections. It depresses the tone of the moral feelings, and hinders the development of piety in Christian souls. When entered upon, it is found to be full of intrigues, petty jealousies, and selfish contentions; while its rewards are the most hollow and illusory that can be imagined.

I will not deny that to be loved and recognized by

the public for a character worthily won, and for services faithfully and unselfishly rendered, is a boon to be gratefully received and genially cherished. An ambition to be worthy of public honor and popular recognition is a legitimate motive of a noble mind. That there are sweet rewards in such a recognition as this, is not to be denied; but a notoriety, sought for its own sake, and attained for purely selfish ends—a public life entered upon for the rewards of fame—is one of the basest things and most miserable cheats in the world. Estimated legitimately, all public life is a private burden, to be assumed as a matter of duty, and borne unselfishly. Such public life as this deserves honor, as one of its incidental rewards, but there is not a worthy mind in the world that occupies a prominent position before the public that does not turn, and return, to the little circle of home and its affections—to the grateful sphere of its private life—for that which is sweetest and best in the material of its earthly happiness.

Grass grows not upon the highway, but by the highway side—in humble pasture-lands, in quiet meadows, and in well-fenced homesteads. Where horses tramp, and wheels roll, and cattle tread, and swine are driven in hungry droves, every thing is foul with dust and offal. It is only on the other side of the fence that the clover blooms, and the daisy nods, and the grass spreads itself, undisturbed, into velvet lawns. It is not where unclean beasts rove freely, and browse at will, that the maize perfects its golden product and the bending tree its fruit, but in secluded fields, where the husbandman works and watches unseen. No more is it in public life that the best affections of our natures blossom, and the little virtues spring and spread to give to life the freshness of velvet verdure. No more is it in public life that a golden character is perfected, and fruit is matured and borne unto eternal life. It is only in private life that the highest development, the purest tastes, the sweetest happiness, and the finest consummations and successes of life are found. To these conclusions reason guides us, and experience holds us.

I have alluded to the desire of women for public life, and in this connection, the subject naturally arises again. With women who desire a public career, the question is one of rights and privileges, as if public life were the grand estate of humanity. With me, it is not a question of rights at all, though, if I were to make it such, I should not find myself greatly at variance with those who maintain the rights of women most stoutly. Abstractly, a woman has a right to be, and to do, what she pleases, but the question is not one of right and privilege. It is a question of duty. I believe that it is the right and privilege of woman to remain in private life, if she choose so to remain. It is not the right of man to shirk public responsibility, if it be laid upon him. Man's physical structure and intellectual constitution—his power to labor and endure—his freedom from the sexual disabilities incident to woman—designate him as the world's worker. While private life is his best sphere and his happiest lot, he may not slip his neck from the yoke of public responsibility. If women were needed in public life, they would be in the same condition—they would have no right to decline public duty; but, in the present constitution of society, they are not needed. Duty, therefore, does not call them into public life, and they have the right and the privilege to remain away from public affairs—a privilege which, if properly estimated by them, would prove to them that, for whatever God has denied to them, and for whatever of hardship He has laid upon them, He has made abundant compensations.

It is strange that, in matters like this, men and women will not receive the testimony of competent experience. There is no worthy public man living who will not testify to the surpassing excellence and charm of private life. The higher a man is raised in public life, the more is he removed from that sympathy with the popular heart which flows from common pursuits and a common condition. The frigid isolation of power, the vexations of popular misconstruction, the jealousy and envy of mean minds, the clash of public duty with private friendship—all these are hard to bear, and there is no sensitive and worthy nature that will not shrink from them. The very best of those whom the world has delighted to honor, turn from the dreary loneliness of their sphere to the simple joys of the private life they have left—to its honest, neighborly friendships, its pure habits, its quiet flow of family life, its freedom from care, and its pleasures, with a yearning memory, and sometimes—nay, often—with a memory which does not fail to lament the loss of a sensibility that ought to be touched to tears.

I am inclined to think that much of this vicious longing for public life and notoriety arises from a vice in the character of the private life in which it is born. I am convinced that much of it would be obviated if private life were all that it should be. Man is a social being, and, in his love of approbation, seeks for the recognition of society. If private life moved in large circles, he would get this recognition, and be content with it; but it is a fact, that private life is too much without congenial relationships. It is essentially selfish, and helps to cherish rather than to destroy the appetite for public life. In looking over the world of public life, and the world of those who are seeking it for its own sake, I think it will be found that a large majority of its men and women are those whose private life is meagre in its rewards, or positively unhappy. I believe that the majority of notoriety-hunters are men and women with uncongenial companions, or with no companions at all, or with an insufficient circle of friends, or with a circle of insufficient friends. If private life were entirely what it should be, this disease would doubtless be greatly abated.

I suppose that no one can read the Evangelists without being impressed with the evident shrinking of the Master from publicity. The performance of many a notable miracle was followed by the command that it should not be published. "See that thou tell no man," was His modest mandate. He preached in the synagogues, on the mountains, and by the water-side, but it was because He had a work to do—a mission to perform. His severest words were for those who prayed at the corners of the streets, and gave their alms to be seen of men. There was nothing meaner in His eyes than the thirst for notoriety, and some of the most charming exhibitions of his character were given in the private circle of His disciples, and in the humble homes of such as Mary and Martha. His public life was a life of service. He had a work to do, and was straitened until it should be accomplished. His was a life of privation and discomfort. With the burden of a public life upon Him, moving among the palaces of Jerusalem and the rural homes of the villages of Judea, it was more than an exhibition of His poverty when He said—"Foxes have holes, and the birds of the air have nests, but the Son of Man hath not where to lay His head."

It will, of course, be useless for me to talk to those who have eaten of the insane root; but to the world of young life, now emerging into manhood and womanhood, something may perhaps be said with profit. There is nothing good in public life, nothing valuable in notoriety, that can compensate for the abandonment of a private sphere those men and women who make the sacrifice. If duty call you to office, or a worthy character and worthy works lift you into public notice, bear the honor well, but grudge the smallest charm that it steals from your private life. Let that be as generous in its conditions and as wide in its sympathies as you can make it, and be sure that in it will be found the truest wealth that the world can give you. Learn to look upon all hunters for notoriety, for notoriety's sake, all itching for public life for the sake of its publicity, all greed for office for the purpose of catching the public eye, with contempt, as the meanest of all mean ambitions. And when you find yourself listening to the suggestions of an ambition like this, regard it as a disease, which only a more worthy and generous private life can cure.

XXIII.

HOME.

"The fire burns brightest on one's own hearth."
"A tree often transplanted neither grows nor thrives."
"He who is far from home is near to harm."
"He who is everywhere is no where."

WIND and water wander round the world, and grow fresher for the journey. The lost diamond knows no difference between the dust where it lies and the bosom from which it fell; but every thing that has vitality requires a home. Every thing that lives seeks to establish permanent relations with that upon which it must depend for supplies. Every plant and every animal has its country, and in that country a favorite location, where it finds that which will give it the healthiest development, and the most luxurious life. Maize will not grow in England, and oranges are not gathered in Lapland. The white bear pines and dies under the equator, and the lion refuses to live in polar latitudes. The elm of a century may not be transplanted with safety, unless a large portion of its home be taken with it. In jungles and dens, in root-beds and parasitic footholds, in rivers, and brooks, and bays, in lakes and seas, in cabins, and tents, and palaces, every thing that lives, from the lowest animal and plant to the lordliest man, has a home—a place, or a region, with whose resources its vitality has established relations. I have no doubt, with analogy only for the basis of my belief, that God, the fountain of life, has a home, and that there is somewhere in space a place which we call heaven.

What is true of all organic material life is equally true of all mental and spiritual life. It is not because the soul is the tenant of a body which must have a home, that it, too, is subjected to a like necessity. The soul is alive, and must feed that it may continue to live, and that it may thrive. It takes root in material things, or in the spiritual facts that invest and permeate them, no less than in society, through multiplied filaments of relation; and its roots may never be violently dislocated without serious damage to its life. Let a man be removed from his accustomed place in the world, and from the society of wife and children, and friends and neighbors, and twenty-four hours will suffice to make him a weaker man, and to institute in him either a general or special process of demoralization. The home-sickness of the Swiss soldier is a genuine disease, with a natural cause which operates independently of his will and beyond his control. The soul that has once adjusted itself to its conditions, and has found the food necessary to nourish its growth and augment its vital wealth, is nearest to its good; and the moment it leaves these conditions for those which are strange, it approaches its evil. Let the accustomed influences which hold it to virtue, and strengthen its power to resist temptation, and nourish its religious life, be escaped from, and it will more readily become the prey of its own evil propensities, and of the demoralizing influences that assail it from without.

These facts find confirmation in familiar popular experience. The influence of vacation and summer travel has been felt by multitudes. Some of our most exemplary men, who have never been known to kick over the traces of propriety at home, break in the dasher and run away with the vehicle at a sea-side hotel. The glass of wine, which never meets their lips at home, is indulged in without alarm among strangers. Bowling alleys and whist tables and billiard rooms, which are considered very bad things when among acquaintances, are transformed into excellent institutions in distant locations. Dignified gentlemen—officers of the church and officers of the state—become boyish and hilarious—not unfrequently uproarous—in an unfamiliar presence. The cords of the moral nature, kept taut in the presence of familiar associates, adapt themselves with marvellous readiness to the prevalent feebleness of tension found in the humid atmosphere of watering places.

Fixedness of location becomes, then, a condition vitally necessary to the growth of a true character, and the preservation of the health and harmony of the functions of the soul. The soul, like the body, lives by what it feeds on. It must increase, or it must diminish. Travel has its benefits, but they are indirect. They come from rest—not from growth. The direct influence of travel is dissipation. No man ever comes back from travel with his powers unimpaired. The power to concentrate the mind, and to perform labor in the accustomed way, is, in a measure, lost, and must be reacquired. Now, if this condition of fixedness be necessary to those who already possess character and Christian principle, how much more necessary is it to those who are mainly held to propriety and virtue by outward influences. The young men who leave Christian homes in the country, go to the city, and, finding the restraints of home removed, plunge into various forms of sin. The young women who gather in boarding-houses, which are so far without a home-character that they are regarded only as places to eat and sleep in, rarely fail of receiving serious moral injury. A con stant traveller who is constantly devout may possibly exist, but I have never seen him. The itinerant professions have never, I believe, been noted for exhibitions of intellectual growth, or profound piety. Gold hunters in California and Australia become in a few months semi-savages. No genuine observer can decide otherwise than that the homes of a nation are the bulwarks of personal and national safety and thrift. A curse upon all those fantastic methods of living, dreamed of by socialism and communism, which would sacrifice home to the meagre economies of great establishments, where humanity is fed in stalls like cattle!

I may legitimately qualify or adapt what I have said so far as to admit that a poor home with a poor location may be exchanged for a better one. A plant may be dislocated from an old, and removed to a new bed, not unfrequently with advantage. It may exhaust the soil where it stands, and demand more room for its roots. I have seen many men greatly improved by transplantation, but the process of adaptation and acclimation through which they were obliged to pass, before they could establish intimate relations with the new soil, was proof of the difficulty and danger of the process. This transplanting process is constantly going on, however, with good results. The wife in the new home is more than the daughter in the old one. New food, new influences, more room, fresh functions are always beckoning us to better locations; but the lives are comparatively few that exhaust a home of medium advantages. The acquisition of a good home is one of the first objects of life—a home where the soul has exclusive rights—a home where it may grow undisturbed, sending out its roots into a fertile society, and lifting up its branches into the sunlight of heaven—a home out from which the soul may go on its errands and enterprises, and to which it may return for its rewards—a home which, along the conduits of memory, may bear pure nourishment to children and children's children while it stands, and even after it has fallen.

I recall a home like this, long since left behind in the journey of life; and its memory floats back over me with a shower of emotions and thoughts toward whose precious fall my heart opens itself greedily like a thirsty flower. It is a home among the mountains—humble and homely—but priceless in its wealth of associations. The waterfall sings again in my ears, as it used to sing through the dreamy, mysterious nights. The rose at the gate, the patch of tansy under the window, the neighboring orchard, the old elm, the grand machinery of storms and showers, the little smithy under the hill that flamed with strange light through the dull winter evenings, the wood-pile at the door, the ghostly white birches on the hill, and the dim blue haze upon the retiring mountains—all these come back to me with an appeal which touches my heart and moistens my eyes. I sit again in the doorway at summer nightfall, eating my bread and milk, looking off upon the darkening landscape, and listening to the shouts of boys upon the hill-side, calling or driving homeward the reluctant herds. I watch again the devious way of the dusty night-hawk along the twilight sky, and listen to his measured note, and the breezy boom that accompanies his headlong plunge toward the earth.

Even the old barn, crazy in every timber and gaping at every joint, has charms for me. I try again the breathless leap from the great beams into the bay. I sit again on the threshold of the widely open doors —open to the soft south wind of spring—and watch the cattle, whose faces look half human to me, as they sun themselves, and peacefully ruminate, while, drop by drop, the dissolving snow upon the roof drills holes through the wasting drifts beneath the eaves, down into the oozing offal of the yard. The first little lambs of the season toddle by the side of their dams, and utter their feeble bleatings, while the flock nibble at the hay rick, or a pair of rival wethers try the strength of their skulls in an encounter, half in earnest and half in play. The proud old rooster crows upon his dunghill throne, and some delighted member of his silly family leaves her nest, and tells to her mates and to me that there is another egg in the world. The old horse whinnies in his stall, and calls to me for food. I look up to the roof, and think of last year's swallows—soon to return again—and hear the tortions of their musical morocco, as it wraps their young, and catch a glimpse of angular sky through the diamond-shaped opening that gave them ingress and egress. How, I know not, and care not, but that old barn is a part of myself—it has entered into my life, and given me growth and wealth.

But I look into the house again, where the life abides which has appropriated these things, and finds among them its home. The hour of evening has come, the lamps are lighted, and a good man in middle life—though very old he seems to me—takes down the well-worn Bible, and reads a chapter from its hallowed pages. A sweet woman sits at his side, with my sleepy head upon her knee, and brothers and sisters are grouped reverently around. I do not understand the words, but I have been told that they are the words of God, and I believe it. The long chapter ends, and then we all kneel down, and the good man prays. I fall asleep with my head in the chair, and the next morning remember nothing of the way in which I went to bed. After breakfast the Bible is taken down, and the good man prays again; and again and again is the worship repeated through all the days of many golden years. The pleasant converse of the fireside, the simple songs of home, the words of encouragement as I bend over my school-tasks, the kiss as I lie down to rest, the patient bearing with the freaks of my restless nature, the gentle counsels mingled with reproofs and approvals, the sympathy that meets and assuages every sorrow and sweetens every little success—all these return to me amid the responsibilities which press upon me now, and I feel as if I had once lived in heaven, and, straying, had lost my way.

Well, the good man grew old and weary, and fell asleep at last, with blessings on his lips for me. Some of those who called him father lie side by side with him in the same calm sleep. The others are scattered, and dwell in new homes, and the old house and barn and orchard have passed into the possession of strangers, who have learned, or are learning, to look back upon them as I do now. Lost, ruined, forever left behind, that home is mine to-day as truly as it ever was, for have I not brought it away with me, and shown it to you? It was the home of my boyhood. In it I found my first mental food, and by it was my young soul fashioned. To me, through weary years, and many dangers and sorrows, it has been a perennial fountain of delight and purifying influences, simply because it was my home, and was and is a part of me. The rose at the gate blooms for me now. The landscape comes when I summon it, and I hear the voices that call to me from lips which memory makes immortal.

Thus the memory of the past joins hands with the experience and observation of to-day, to illustrate and enforce the philosophy which I have propounded. A homeless man, or a man hopeless of home, is a ruined man. A man who, in the struggles of life, has no home to retire to, in fact or in memory, is without life's best rewards and life's best defences. Away from home, shut off from the income of those influences which feed his life—from those relations along which the life of God is accustomed to flow to him—a man stands exactly where evil will the most readily get the mastery of him. A man is always nearest to his good when at home, and farthest from it when away.

One of the very first duties of life, I say again, is the establishment of a home which shall be to us and to our children the fountain and reservoir of our best life; and this home should be a permanent one, if possible. Home is the centre of every true life, the place where all sweet affections are brought forth and nurtured, the spot to which memory clings the most fondly, and to which the wanderer returns the most gladly. It is worth a life of care and labor to win for ourselves, and the dear children whom we love as ourselves, a home whose influence shall enrich us and them while life lasts. God pity the poor child who cannot associate his youth with some dear spot where he drank in life's freshness, and shaped the character he bears!

The choosing of a home is one of the most momentous steps a man is ever called upon to make. If we plant a tree with the hope to sit some time beneath its shadow, and eat of its fruit, we do not plant it in the sand, or in a stream of running water. It is astonishing to see the multitudes that thoughtlessly plant their homes in moral and intellectual deserts—to see them building houses where there is no society, or only that which is bad, where the church-bell is never heard, and where a fertile and fruitful home-life is absolutely impossible. For money men will rush from the healthful and pleasant country village to the feverish and stony city, or forsake a thousand privileges that are valuable beyond all price, and settle in a wilderness where the degeneration of their home is certain. Circumstances may force one into locations like these, but they can only be regarded as calamitous. Communion is the law of growth, and homes only thrive where they sustain relations with each other.

The sweetest type of heaven is home—nay, heaven itself is the home for whose acquisition we are to strive the most strongly. Home, in one form and another, is the great object of life. It stands at the end of every day's labor, and beckons us to its bosom;

and life would be cheerless and meaningless, did we not discern across the river that divides it from the life beyond, glimpses of the pleasant mansions prepared for us.

XXIV.

LEARNING AND WISDOM.

"A mere scholar at court is an ass among apes."
"A handful of common sense is worth a bushel of learning."
"Wisdom does not always speak in Greek and Latin."
"A man must sell his ware at the rate of the market."

THE intrinsic value of learning, as a possession and a power, is exhibited most remarkably, perhaps, in a man who knows every thing, and is nothing. He may be likened to a pond full of water, without an outlet. The water is all very well in itself, though none the better for being stagnant. A few lazy lily-pads may seek the sun upon its surface, but its chief office is to drink old starlight, to entertain the shadows of the tall trees that grow upon its banks, and to receive them when they fall. If it can be artificially tapped, for the purpose of feeding some literary institution, as the Bostonians have tapped the Cochituate, it is very well; and this seems to be about the only use it can be appropriated to. Very unlike this is the learning that has a natural, common-sense delivery, through a stream that carries out into the world, full and free, its aggregated crystal, to feed the roots of flowers and grasses, and slake the thirst of flocks and herds, and torture the sunshine as it slides down rocky rapids, and turn the mill-wheel that grinds the corn and weaves the fabrics of the poor, and

"Repeat the music of the rain"

at the feet of plashy waterfalls, and join and mingle in the river of human action that sweeps on to fill the ocean of human achievement. I do not think that it can be said, truthfully, that learning possesses intrinsic, independent value, or that it has power, in and of itself, to make a man either valuable to himself or the world. Learning may as well lie dormant in dead books as in dead men. I would as soon have a library that costs nothing, after purchase, but the dusting, as a learned man who eats and drinks and wears respectable broadcloth. In fact, the library is more ornamental and less troublesome than the man, and is not always painfully reminding one that it might possibly have made a good tin-peddler if it had begun early enough in life.

I am aware that this is not the usual view of this

subject. Some, perhaps, assent to it rationally, but practically it is hardly entertained at all. The pupil in the humblest school is estimated entirely according to his capacity to cram into his mental maw and retain the facts in philosophy, science, and history set before him. Memory is every thing; reason, thorough intellectual digestion, and symmetrical intellectual development, are nothing. This runs up the whole grade of educational institutions, and comes to a head not unfrequently on Commencement days, when the ass of a class pronounces the valedictory, to subside into nonentity, and the really educated man leaves without an appointment, and with the pitying contempt of the Faculty, to win the world's prizes, reflect honor upon the college, and to take rank among the intellectual giants of his time. Learning and education are widely deemed identical things and synonymous words. Consequently we have among the learned, in a work-a-day world like this, constant surprises. They find themselves shelved, laid aside, left behind, while the unlearned take their places in the world's eye, in the world's heart, and in the world's work. Cobblers represent a state full of colleges in the national councils, machinists become brilliant speakers and wise governors, and country merchants stand at the head of educational systems that embrace the growing mind of a state. All the developments of the age serve to illustrate the superiority of wisdom and common sense to mere learning, and the utter worthlessness of all learning, when dissociated from those qualities and powers which can bring it into relation with the practical questions and every-day life of the time.

I am not seeking to depreciate learning, but to define its real value and its only value. It has stood in the way of the world's progress, almost as much as it has contributed to it. Its tendency is to worship the old—to abide within the bounds of old formularies invented by a less developed life than ours, to look chaos-ward for light instead of millennium-ward, to seek for truth among the broken fountains of the schools rather than at truth's own fountain, to follow in the track of old systems grown too narrow for the expanding life of the present, and to enchain itself with the bonds of old creeds and old philosophies. The spirit of learning, particularly as manifested through the learned professions, is an arrogant, self-sufficient, self-complacent, and proscriptive spirit. It lays its ban on all schemes of improvement, all experimental search for truth, all speculation in the field of thought, which itself does not originate. All trade carried on outside its marts is contraband. It calls unlearned thinkers "quacks," indiscriminately. All systems of philosophy and art, of which it is not the father, are illegitimate.

Medicine is a "learned profession," and its learning

has been converted into its bane. It is bound to its books, and its formulas, and its unreasoning routine with a devotion so insane, that its professors band themselves in societies by which every member is kept to his creed through fear of proscription, and by which all outside experimenters in the healing art, however truth-loving, ingenious and scientific, are professionally and socially damned. Any man who leaps out of the regular old professional frying-pan, alights in a fire of professional malediction. It is all a regular physician's reputation is worth to seek for truth out of the well-trodden, regular channels, particularly if the new channels have become objects of professional prejudice and jealousy. The consequence of this is, of course, to retard the progress of medicine as a healing art. Medical learning has absolutely fought against every great medical discovery, and not unfrequently against important discoveries in the constituent sciences. All other arts have advanced within the last century beyond calculation. It has been a century of progress in art and discovery in science; but we look in vain for those advances in medical science and art which place them even-footed with their thrifty sisterhood.

Let me not be misapprehended in these statements. I am neither talking about nor against any system of medicine. I am simply condemning that arrogant spirit of professionally associated learning, which assumes the monopoly of all that is truly known of the subject of medicine, and the privilege and right of making all changes and discoveries in medical art and science. I condemn the spirit which refuses to see, and hear, and consider, and treat respectfully, all truth, by whatever man discovered—from whatever source it may proceed. I condemn the spirit which makes a man a bond-slave to a system devised by other men, and whose prominent effect is to create more reverence for authority than for truth. I condemn the spirit which sets learning above wisdom and common sense. I condemn the spirit which, in effect, binds men to a blind, unreasoning routine, and forbids their entrance into the field of intelligent, rational experiment. I condemn the spirit which makes medical heterodoxy a social crime, to be punished by social proscription. I condemn the spirit which is the principal hindrance to the development of the noblest, most humane, most useful, and most important of all the arts.

The law, too, is a learned profession, whose only legitimate office is to promote the ends of justice among men, and whose constant practice is to pervert justice, or prevent it, by resort to the technicalities and forms with which it is hide-bound. There is no department of human interest that is so full of the lumber—the old dead stuff—of learning, as the law. A simple matter of justice between man and man would seem to be a simple matter to adjudicate, on a competent representation of facts. It would seem to be a matter easily to be handled and quickly disposed of; but learning resorts to forms for delay, and picks flaws in forms for escape, and hunts among maggots for precedents, and bewilders with the array of authority, until that which is simple becomes complicated, and an affair of thirty minutes becomes a thing of ten years. I have such a respect for the law, that I believe that if every law and law-book ever written were smitten from existence, the honest, common-sense lawyers of to-day could frame codes of law and rules for their administration that would shorten and cheapen the processes of justice by the amount of nine-tenths. I believe that every lawyer believes this, yet he allows this rotten, cumbersome conglomeration of relics of effete institutions, and products of defunct ingenuities, to warp, and mould, and modify his nature, till he becomes a slave of authority and precedent in every thing, with red tape in every button-hole, and a green bag on his head.

Religion is a simple thing, so simple that "a wayfaring man, though a fool, need not err therein." The only fountain of religious truth is the Bible. We have it in our native tongue, and many a simple soul, without the aid of clergyman or schoolman, has drawn from it the inspiration of a new life and all the instruction that he needed touching his relations to God and men. Yet theology—human invention and human learning—has made religion a very complicated thing. It has elevated dogma, and creed, and formulary into prominence, and debased love and life into obscurity. It in sists more on faith in tenets than in God, and denies to a Christian spirit the fellowship which it accords to rational belief. The disgraceful wrangles of the religious newspapers, the great disputes of the schools, and the high controversies of the pulpit and the pamphlet, are the quarrels and strifes for mastery of theologians, not Christians—of learning, not love. Theology clings to old words and phrases after their life has departed. Theology is arrogant, selfish, and proud. Theology excludes from the table of the Lord those whom He has accepted. Theology denies fellowship and communion to those whom Love expects to meet in Heaven. Theology casts out of the synagogue those who rise to think, while Christ forgives those who stoop to sin, and, without condemnation, bids them sin no more. Theology builds rival churches, pits against each other rival sects, and wastes God's money. I believe that it would be every way better for the world, if every book of dogmatic and controversial theology could be blotted out of existence, and Christendom were obliged to begin anew, drawing every thing from the great Book of Books, leaving Paul and Apollos, and Princeton, and New Haven, and Cambridge, behind.

and learning of Him "who spake as never man spake."

The long and short of the matter is, that the learned world has become so deeply involved in the thoughts of those who have gone before—so accustomed to following old channels, and to paying reverence to the opinions and systems of schools, that it cannot step out freely into the field of truth and handle things as it finds them. The common sense that deals with things instead of systems which treat of them, and the wisdom which grows out of this intimate contact and loving association with the actualities of human life and experience, are worth more to the world than all the learning in it. This handling of the vital realities of to-day with the gloves of dead men; this slow dragging of the trains of the present over old grass-grown turnpikes; this old monopoly of power and privilege among interests that touch every individual—the highest and the humblest; this stopping of the wheels of progress, at every toll-gate and frontier, for the benefit of learned publicans, is certainly against the common sense of the world, as it undoubtedly is against "the spirit of the age," if anybody knows exactly what that is. Any thing and every thing which places fetters upon the spirit of inquiry, which blinds the eyes of discovery, and abridges the freedom of thought, whether it be contained in the lore of past ages or of the present time, is a thing to be contemned and abjured. A living man with a carcase lashed to his back may creep but he cannot run.

Learning runs back for every thing, and reaches forward for nothing. It educates the young Christian mind of to-day by leading it through a literature whose highest inspirations were found in paganism. It seeks for models of style and expression among authors enthroned among the classical, who only became worthy of the distinction by laying their hearts by the side of Nature, that realm which is spread all around us now, illuminated with Christian light, yet forsaken for second-hand sources of instruction. It ignores the theory and the fact of human progress, and reverses the order of nature by making an old world obedient to a young world.

But I stay too long from the definition of the legitimate sphere and real value of learning. Whenever learning becomes tributary to wisdom, it occupies its legitimate sphere, and by the amount of its tribute is it valuable. The soul that abides in learning as an end—that pursues learning as an end—that finds in it food, raiment, and guidance—that surrenders itself to the records of other minds, perverts learning and perverts itself. The soul that uses learning as a means by which to project itself into a higher life—that stands upon it, with all its truth and all its falsehood, as upon a platform from which it may survey a better truth and a nobler issue—uses learning aright, and is enriched. The future is an untrodden realm. Around each step, as the world advances, new circumstances will gather, new emergencies arise, new problems present themselves for solution. With these circumstances, emergencies, and problems, the common sense and wisdom of the world are to deal, and not the world's learning. We do not repeat through unvarying cycles the experiences of the past. Comparatively little of the records of life and thought of the ages that are gone can have direct relation to the ages that are to come. If the learned men of the present find themselves left behind in the race of life, it is simply and only because, while they have been walking among graves, or busying themselves with facts for which the real life of the world has no use, the wisdom and common sense of the world have got in advance of them. A man must sell his ware at the rate of the market, not only, but he must supply the market with what it demands.

But learning has a noble value. It is like the mould that accumulates from the decay of each succeeding year of vegetation. It furnishes a humus into which the roots of mental and moral life may penetrate for nourishment, but out of which that life must spring and mount into the air and sunlight. Human life is not a potato—a bloated tuber that battens in the muck of other times, but a stalk of maize, burdened with golden fruitage, and whispering through all its leaves of the life within it and the influences without it. It is not a thing whose issue and end are in its roots, but in a life to which those roots are tributary; and all the learning which may not be assimilated to that life is as valueless as the dust of its authors.

XXV.

RECEIVING AND DOING.

"Virtue consists in action."
"He who does no more than another, is no better than another."
"Let not him who has a mouth ask another to blow."
"Do good if you expect to receive good."

THERE is no healthy physical life without a proper balance of the active and receptive habitudes of the body. If a man eat too much and act too little, he will become gross and gouty, or dull and dyspeptic. If he act too much and eat too little, he will be weak and inefficient, or spasmodic and irascible. It is not enough to eat; it is not enough to work; but eating and working should go hand in hand—the first being sufficient to supply the vital expenditure, and the vital expenditure being sufficient to exhaust the supply furnished by the food. By this balance, the digestive functions are kept sharp and healthy, and the muscular organs are developed to the measure of their power. The man who eats much and works little is necessarily a stupid man; but the man who expends in labor what he has received in food, in a legitimate way, finds himself, under favorable conditions, the possessor of a happy and a healthy life.

We can have no better illustration than this of the necessity to healthy mental life of the preservation of a proper balance between the active and receptive attitudes and habitudes of the mind. The mind that imagines that its grand good is to be achieved while in its receptive attitude—that is bent on receiving and acquiring—will find itself greatly mistaken; yet the theory of education is mainly the theory of acquiring, and contemplates almost entirely a receptive habit. The honors paid to simple learning are tributes to the faculty and fact of mental stuffing. A large proportion of the very learned men of the world are those who really do nothing for themselves or their race—who are not recognized as powers in society, and whose simplicity, lack of common sense, and inability to take care of themselves, make them the laughing-stock of boys who have ciphered through the Rule of Three, and learned to look out for number one. There is a curse on all intellectual gormandizing—all reception of mental food that is not made tributary to mental power. An individual who is simply a man of learning

—whose life has been expended in acquisition—is no man at all. A man of science who does not go out from books into discovery, or who does not aim to apply his knowledge to practical life, or who does not become active in organizing and imparting the knowledge he has acquired, must become intellectually an invalid, or an imbecile.

This is an age of reading, and I am glad that it is; but there is a great deal of reading that is as much mental dissipation as there is eating that is a waste of bodily power. Newspapers, books, and magazines, are devoured by the cargo, for which the devourers render no return, and from which they gain no strength. A great reader—a constant and universal reader—is rarely a good worker. A receptive habit of mind, that can only find satisfaction in devouring, without digesting, illimitable print, is mental death to a man. It is essential dissipation, opposed alike to healthy mental life and development, and positive usefulness in the world. This perfect balance between reception and action—between acquiring and doing—cannot be disturbed in the mental any more than in the muscular world, without bringing with it disease and imbecility.

The facts that I have stated with regard to the body and the mind are important enough in themselves to call for exhibition, but they serve to illustrate, with peculiar force, the dangers of the receptive habit that prevails in the realm of spiritual things. It is no less an age of preaching than of reading. All over this land congregations of uncounted thousands go up every Sunday to be played upon by sermons—to have their intellects quickened, their sympathies excited, their imaginations inspired, and their whole spiritual natures acted upon by their preacher. They want a morning sermon, and an afternoon sermon, and many of them would be glad to have an evening sermon. They go to their weekly prayer-meeting, and would always be glad to have a sermon there. They love to have their hearts raked open and stirred up by an eloquent exhortation, or melted by the pathos of a touching prayer. Their hearts are not only open and crying for more from the preacher, but they are open toward God, and crying to Him for more. They thirst for the influx of divine influences that shall elevate their spiritual frame. Receptive always, thirsting and hungering always, always eating and drinking, they become thoroughly dissipated in religion, their spiritual life degenerates into an emotional form, and so they become unfitted for Christian action.

I have known multitudes of good and pure people who were almost utterly useless in the world, and powerless in themselves, by remaining for years in this strictly receptive attitude. I have known multitudes who go to a prayer-meeting to have a good time, precisely the same as others would go to a ball to have a good time. Their religious exercises have become a sort of holy amusement. They go to be stirred and refreshed, to have their emotions excited, and to receive something which shall make them feel. They care not so much to learn how to do better as to be made to feel better. Exaltation of emotion—spiritual intoxication—is the object mainly sought for. Woe be to the preacher if he fail so to act upon them as to procure the fulfilment of this object. It will not be enough that he lay down the law and line of duty with faithfulness, and spend his days in visits and labors of sympathy and love. He must preach with power; he must pour forth with abundance; he must bring stimulating draughts to the greedy lips of decaying emotions, or he will be proscribed.

It is precisely thus with the music of the sanctuary. The number of hearts that go up actively in a song of praise, in a congregation of five hundred persons, is very small. Hearts and ears are thrown open to drink in the influence of the music, as if the congregation, and not God, were addressed by the hymn. In the minds of too many ministers prayer itself is something to be addressed in about equal parts to the congregation and to the Most High. It is regarded not altogether as the vehicle for aspiration and petition, but as a portion of the machinery by which their people are to be moved. I have heard theology, exhortation, and even personal condemnation mingled with addresses to the throne—not unfrequently a whole family history. It is hard sometimes to tell a sermon from a prayer. If ministers so far forget the proprieties of prayer as to prostitute it to the purposes of declamation, the people may well talk of "eloquent prayers," and of men "gifted in prayer," and forget that it is God and not themselves who is the object addressed. Thus it is that nearly all the "means of grace," technically speaking, contemplate a receptive attitude on the part of the people. They are preached to, sung to, prayed to; and, as the preaching and singing and praying are calculated to feed their emotional natures, or otherwise, are they satisfied or dissatisfied.

Now the whole tendency of this thing is to spiritual debility and imbecility. Some of the most inefficient churches in this country are those which have what is called great preaching, and "splendid music." They enjoy their Sabbath; they have most refreshing seasons of communion, they hold delightful prayer-meetings, and imagine that all is right with them, while they see no results of good to others around them, and wonder at it. How long must the world live before the Christian church will learn that its power in the world depends on what it does, and not on what it feels? How long must the church live before it will learn that strength is won by action, and success by work, and that all this immeasurable feeding without action and work is a positive damage to it—that it is the procurer of spiritual obesity, gout, and debility?

The world of Christian life wants to be turned squarely around, and be made to assume a new attitude. The world is never to be converted by Christian feeling. What difference will it make with my careless neighbor that I have enjoyed a fine sermon, if it do not move me to efforts for his good? What will it avail my sweet friend who languishes upon her death-bed that my sympathies have been played upon by eloquent 'ips, if they do not lead me to her bedside with offices of kindness and words of cheer? Why and how is the world better for the powerful representation to me of the claims of Christianity, if it do not stir me up to the work of gathering and saving the neglected little ones who are growing into a vicious and ignorant manhood and womanhood? Am I selfishly to congratulate myself that I have obtained new views of the divine nature and the divine love, without zealously endeavoring to bring the dumb and dead souls around me to the same recognition? "He that does no more than another is no better than another." Life has language always. Expression is the natural offspring of possession. If my life and my spiritual possessions exceed the measure of another man, they will demonstrate their superiority in action. If my humane but unchristian neighbor do more good than I do, then his humanity, as a motive principle of life, is better than my Christianity.

There are three distinct aspects in which Christian action may be viewed with propriety and profit. The first relates to spiritual development. There can be no growth of power, in any faculty of the soul, or any combination of faculties, without use. Action is the law and condition of spiritual development, as it is of muscular development. That which we try to do, and persist in doing, becomes easy to do, not because its nature is changed, but because our power to do is developed. Christian beneficence is a grace that grows by cultivation. A man who is accustomed to give is the man who gives freely and gladly. An excellent thing for spiritual plethora is the bleeding of the pocket-book. It is only those who do—who act—that become powers in the Christian world. A man may hear a hundred and fifty sermons in a year, and five hundred prayers and as many hymns, and be melted and stirred and exalted by them, and still be a spiritual baby, without nerve, or faculty, or power, and even without having learned any thing practically. It is only those who do their duty that learn the doctrine aright. It is only those who come into contact with human nature and human condition in the work of Christianity that learn and appreciate its relation to that nature and condition. We know the truth of a principle by applying it in practice. The principle of Davy's saiety lamp may be received as true, but it is not known to be true till the lamp is made and used. We accept the proposition that it is more blessed to give than to receive, but we know nothing about it, until we try it and demonstrate it. It is in the line of duty that all the highest truth becomes incorporated into the soul's knowledge. A Christian who does nothing is not only undeveloped as a man of power, but he absolutely knows nothing. All truth is to be digested, assimilated, developed into life, before it really becomes a possession—no less than before it becomes a power.

The second aspect in which Christian action may be viewed is that which relates to the outside world. In the development of the subject this has already been touched upon, but more remains to be said. It is a notorious and well-recognized fact that, considering the agencies engaged in the Christian work, the results are small. I place the responsibility for these insignificant results upon the constantly receptive and persistently inactive position of the church itself. There was never so much good preaching, praying, and singing in the world as r ow. There was never a more general disposition to 'go to meeting." The Christian ministry were never so put up to the exhibi tion of every faculty within them as in this age. It is all feeding, feeding, feeding. It is all ministry to the greedy flock. We pay better salaries than we used to, and expect more for the money, yet we grow dead and dumb from year to year. The church is not generally aggressive. Now and then, here and there, it becomes active, and immediately there springs up a great reformation, but the lesson is unheeded, and we go on gorging and gormandizing, and wonder why nothing comes of it but increasing weakness and a growing disposition to inaction.

It is not enough that the Christian give his money to feed the poor, and sustain efforts for the reclamation of the vicious, and send the Gospel to the heathen, and support the church at home. The money is wanted, and there must be a more general opening of the purse-strings before very great things will be accomplished· but more than all is wanted direct personal effort on the part of the church. Everywhere a Christian should be a positive power, distinctly pronounced in some way, so that wherever he carries himself, he will carry the power of Christianity. The world says "what does he more than others?" of the constantly receptive Christian, and entertains a contempt as damaging as it is just for all those Christians who do nothing.

The opinion that the world entertains of a man's Christianity is usually a just one. It is rarely far from right. It is perfectly legitimate to say of a man who professes to be a Christian, and gives no evidence in his life and influence of the possession of Christianity as a motive power, that his religion is vain.

It is not only essential to an undefiled religion, that a man keep himself unspotted from the world, but he must visit the widows and the fatherless—demonstrate the life in him by ministry. When the church shall become active, and leave behind its laziness and languor, and seek for food that it may have more power to work, and expend the strength it gets, the world will be converted, and it is pretty safe to say that it will not before.

The third aspect in which Christian action may be viewed, contemplates its relations to God himself. Many a man conscientiously goes up to the weekly pulpit-feeding, through storm and sickness, as a matter of duty, who never thinks of doing a work of Christian mercy, or engaging in any kind of ministry during the week. Sometimes a considerable sacrifice of time and convenience is made, in order to attend the weekly prayer-meeting, by those who manage to keep themselves comfortable in their consciences only by this means. Now the Christian world knows its duty well enough. It has no need of half the teaching it gets. It is always feeding beyond its necessities, and, as I honestly believe, to its own damage. Let it ask itself which would please its Master best—teaching some ignorant child the way of life, or going to hear a great sermon—visiting and consoling some poor mourner, or going to a prayer-meeting—stirring up some weak soul to duty, or seeking for an hour of emotional excitement—going to meeting always, or laboring occasionally for the reclamation of some sad wanderer from the path of virtue?

Considering the amount of good which the church has received, how great a return has it rendered? What is it doing, and what has it done, outside of its own immediate necessities? It hires ministers, and pays for tracts, and contents itself with the acquisition of a cartilaginous and an oleaginous spirit and life. Oh, for bone and muscle, and blood and nerve, and courage and power! Is religion one of the fine arts, that it should consist in going to meeting in good clothes every Sunday, saying grace at table, and praying night and morning? Is there every thing to receive, and nothing to give? Are we so literally a flock that we have nothing to do but to be fed all the year, yielding only the annual fleece which forms our pastor's salary? Practically this is the popular Christian notion, but how miserably unworthy it is!

Action, then, is alike the condition of the development of Christian life as it relates to the Christian himself, of aggressiveness as it relates to the world, and of appropriate return for benefits received. Religion is not a thing of emotion exclusively, nor even mainly. It is a motive power of life in all beneficent directions toward man, and in all devotional ways toward God. It is a life of reception in one aspect, and a life of action in another. Of him to whom much is given much is required. Every imbibition of truth and every influx of spiritual life is to thrill along the nerves, and invade the veins, of the soul's faculties, and find manifestation in action. Emotion, feeling—these are well enough if they feed the springs of power. Prayer, praise, preaching—these are all good, and never to be dispensed with; but if the life to which they minister have no manifestation out of them, it is a failure.

XXVI.

THE SECRET OF POPULARITY.

"Self-love is a mote in every man's eye."
"If you love yourself overmuch, nobody else will love you at all."
"If I sleep, I sleep for myself; if I work, I know not for whom."
"The way to be admired is to be what we love to be thought."

THERE is a class of men in every community that, more than any other class, desires popularity, and less than any other class gets it. They may be men of pleasant address and honorable dealing, but there is something about them that repels the popular sympathy. If the people were to be questioned as to the reasons of their antipathy, they would, in most instances, find it difficult to make an intelligent answer. They would say with Tom Brown:—

"I do not love thee, Doctor Fell;
The reason why I cannot tell,
But this alone I know full well—
I do not love thee, Doctor Fell!"

The unfailing heart recognizes an unworthy and repulsive element in these men, though the intellect may fail to comprehend it. Now, if the intellect will make direct inquiry, it will find that these lovers of popularity are supremely selfish—that they love themselves better than any thing, or anybody else, and that all the popularity they long for and seek for is demanded by their self-love. They are not men of generous impulses, but of cool and painstaking calculation. If they make a gift, it is for a purpose. A policy that has its centre in self overrules all their actions.

This element of popularity in a man's character is very little understood. On looking about us, we shall find the popular favor bestowed with comparatively little reference to personal character. Many a man, known to be immoral, will have troops of friends, while a multitude of others, of whom nothing bad can be said, will have the affections of no man.

These facts show me how closely, side by side, the better intuitions and instinctive judgments of the world stand with the central principle of Christianity. The world, no less than Christianity—the great human heart, no less than the true religion—demands that men shall be unselfish before they receive personal affection and favor. Religion asks for more than unselfishness, because it lays its claims upon personal character and personal devotion, but it starts at that, as the initial point. The world asks that a man shall be generous from natural impulse, and not from any special principle or policy. It is often that these impulsively generous men are impulsively vicious, yet this does not always, nor often, repel even the good from sympathy with them. We love some men in spite of ourselves. Our judgment condemns them, our religious feelings are offended by them; yet the one element of good which they possess receives our admiration and our homage, and we return their cordial grip and greeting impulsively, and protest only in secret leisure.

All of us love to stand well with our fellows. We thirst for popular esteem, and rejoice in popular good-will. This desire for popularity is universal, though it has its birth in widely various motives; but it is never satisfied save when it is called forth by and to generous natures. The whole world loves Florence Nightingale, simply because she unselfishly sacrificed the ease and comfort of a luxurious home, for the purpose of ministering to the wants of the sick and wounded soldiers. Half of the world's admiration of Jenny Lind grows out of her characteristic benevolence. The rough fireman who braves the dangers of a burning house, to save the life of some helpless inmate, is regarded as a hero, and we toss up our cap as he goes by us. The man or the woman who, from a generous impulse, risks danger and death for others, or who, from a similar impulse, becomes the subject of suffering or inconvenience that others may be benefited, compels the homage of every cognizant heart.

If we love ourselves overmuch, nobody else will love us at all. We cannot get the world's esteem without paying for it in advance; and even then our sacrifices will avail nothing unless they are made without reference to the object of gaining popularity. The world has an insight into motives which easily detects the calculating element in all beneficence and all generous doing. It is the native, impulsive, uncalculating generosity of a deed that kindles our admiration—the doing good without reference to consequences that inspires our love. We demand that a good deed, to be the subject of our admiration, shall be the spontaneous offspring of an unselfish, chivalrous heart. The meanest man in the world admires magnanimity—the stingiest, uncalculating generosity—although he may feel himself incapable of their exercise—just as a man physically weak admires a commanding personal prowess, and a coward a deed of daring. So the tribute to generous, unselfish, gallant doing, is universal.

A thing which is so good and admirable in universal human judgment is certainly something which demands a careful consideration, especially as in it abides the secret of this universally coveted good-will. The world declares that selfishness is mean, and unselfishness, generosity, and magnanimity are noble and admirable. This decision cannot be altered, and ought not to be. A man whose plans have reference only to himself is a contemptible man. We neither love him nor trust him. The man who says—"If I sleep, I sleep for myself; if I work, I know not for whom," is a man whom all hearts despise—instinctively and inevitably despise. It matters not how selfish a man may be, there is something in him which tells him that the selfishness he sees in others is contemptible.

I say, then, that the universal judgment is right upon this point, and that it indorses the Christian doctrine that selfishness is the central motive power of sin. Now, there is not a soul in the world that admires a selfish nature. So far, the human mind is unperverted; and no healthy mind can conceive how God can admire such a nature. If I, with my low instincts and perverted tastes, demand that a man shall be, or become unselfish, before I love him, how can I conceive that God will love his unchanged character? I know that He cannot, any more than I can, and I am prepared to take His definition of the sum and substance of religion as the loving of God supremely, and the loving of our neighbor as ourselves. Wrapped within this word *unselfishness*, in its full and glorious meaning, lies the central principle of Christianity, and from it always unfolds the true Christian life. When God sits supremely on the throne of a human heart—I say supremely—then selfishness is obliterated, and the individual becomes small and insignificant in the presence of the great brotherhood.

I suppose it may be stated as a generally admitted truth that mankind are not popular. In other words, the race is not held in very high estimation by itself. If this were not so, David's declaration that all men were liars, was not so very hasty after all; for, if there be a habit everywhere and in all times prevalent, it is the habit of detraction. Mankind are pretty universally unpopular, or universally malignant, for they have a very bad reputation among themselves. I think there is some cause for all this hard talk about men which the most of us indulge in, and that though many uncharitable things may be said, the unjust things are not so plenty. I think that this selfishness of which we have been talking is very common—in fact, that very few of us can lay claim to any great degree of freedom from it. I think that one great reason why we do not love our neighbors better, and why our neighbors do not love us better, is that they and we are not altogether lovable. I think that the great bar to a quicker and higher development of our social life is the contempt we feel for one another's selfishness. If all my neighbors were free-hearted, generous, magnanimous, unselfish men, I should love them all as I may happen to love one of them who manifests the possession of these qualities; and if I were the possessor of these qualities which I most admire in others, I should be sure that all my neighbors who know me would love me.

Christianity, starting in God's fatherhood, bids us love our brotherhood. If we love Him, we shall love His children, however widely straying and however unamiable, simply because they are members of the same family with ourselves. We are nowhere commanded to love the devil and his angels, because they do not belong to our family. But Christianity does not demand that we shall admire an unlovely man, and choose him as a companion, and be happy in his society. It does not demand that I give him a good name, while I seek to do him good, or conspire to hold him popular while I strive to make him better. It does not bid me smother my antipathies so far as to ignore his selfishness, or to accept him as a grateful object of my affections. I can love him so far as to wish him well, to labor for his welfare, and to rejoice in his improvement; can love him in such a manner as to be grateful for all the good he receives and achieves; but, so long as selfishness is dominant in his heart and life, I am not required to delight in him, and I could not if I were. The heart leaps to receive a worthy love, and will not be counselled.

The secret of the world's unloveliness abides in its selfishness. This statement, true in the largest sense, is equally true in its most limited application. The reason why men are not popular with their fellows, is, that their fellows fail to find in them generous, uncalculating impulses—open hearts, free hands, and demonstrative good-will. I have no doubt that this statement will come to many minds either as a new and strange revelation of truth, or as a proposition which their overweening self-love will compel them to quarrel with. I know there are men who are conscious of not being generally loved, and yet, who, having strong desires to be loved, are at a loss to account for their own unpopularity. If they accept this doctrine, they can find the way to win what they desire. If they reject it, as a thing which wounds their self-love and offends them, they can have the privilege of being despised while they live. God has made selfishness unlovable, and shaped the universal human heart to despise it, and He has made unselfishness so lovable that we cannot withhold from it our admiration.

Here comes in the power of Christianity as the transformer of character, and the agent of those changes in the human heart and life, which make men not only lovely to each other, but to God Himself. To my mind, there is no stronger evidence of the truth and divine authenticity of Christianity, than the direct blow with which it hits the nail of human selfishness on the head. There is no other system of religion which does this. There is no curative scheme of human philosophy which even attempts this transformation. No outside plan of reformation, even when it has recognized selfishness as the root of human evil, has been able to present motives of sufficient power to work the necessary regeneration. Under the influence of Christianity, I have seen selfish men become large-hearted and generous, and have witnessed the outgoing of their lives into deeds of practical good-will. I have never seen this change wrought by any other system of religion, nor by any form of human philosophy. All other systems and schemes fail to supply the vital principle of a true life and an admirable character. They are systems and schemes of policy, and plans of rewards and punishments, built upon what is good in humanity. They never contemplate the subversion of the central principle of selfishness in the heart, and the substitution of the principle of benevolence.

As a student of human nature, and an observer of the forces brought to bear upon it, I am compelled to give this tribute to Christianity. There is either in it a combination of powerful motives, rationally to be apprehended and voluntarily to be adopted, or a new principle of life, which, infused into the heart, diffuses itself through every artery and vein, and changes that life's issues. It is not necessary for me to say which I think it is. I only say that there has never been found any transforming and reforming agency equal to it; and that I believe it is the only reliable agency in the world's transformation. It is this which is to make the world altogether lovely like its Founder, who gave His whole life to us—gave it out of His overflowing love and His unselfish nature. As "self-love is a mote in every man's eye," there is no man who does not need to acquire this principle of the Christian life, to make him more loving and lovely. The heart given to the Father, the hand given to the brother, the life given to both—truly this makes a man admirable! Can we resist loving him?

If the instinctive judgments of men coincide with and uphold the Christian standard of loveliness, so do they go further, and reveal to us what the character of that transformation must be which Christianity works in the heart and life. It is not enough that a deed be beneficent in its results, to secure my homage and admiration. I must see that the heart out of which it came was a generous heart—that that heart was moved by hearty sympathy and uncalculating benevolence. I must see no selfish end consulted, no reluctant bending to a sense of obligation, no hard yielding to a conviction of duty. It must be spontaneous—an outburst of noble, generous life. This, my judgment tells me, is admirable, and only this. Now Christianity never works its perfect work in the heart until the outgoings of that heart are of this character. I am not bound to admire, and I cannot admire, a man who, professing to be moved by Christian motives, manifests his life by deeds of benevolence that start in a sense of Christian duty and Christian obligation. The Christian life must be as uncalculating and as spontaneous as the natural life, before its expression can touch my admiration by its quality.

The true heart is just as unerring in its judgment of what constitutes true Christianity as true humanity. Before it will yield its tribute of admiration and affection to him who does a deed of good, it demands that, in either case, there shall be no selfish consideration of any kind. It demands that Christianity shall be as spontaneous and chivalrous as humanity, and it knows that when it is not, it is not the genuine article. Obligation implies the idea of justice. The fulfilment of it is the payment of a debt. Duty is a thing rationally apprehended and intellectually measured. Unselfish benevolence—natural, or acquired by the possession of the Christian life—blossoms with spontaneous beauty, and it is that which we love and which God loves.

So the secret of being loved is in being lovely, and the secret of being lovely is in being unselfish. No man liveth to himself, and no man was made to live to himself. He was born with a desire for the good-will of others, and with the fact (veiled, perhaps, in many instances) looking him in the face, that it is impossible to get it without the relinquishment of selfishness as the ruling motive of his life. The truth is, that the curse of selfishness is upon pretty much all our life. It blackens and defiles every thing. We have not popular men enough to fill decently the offices of government. They are so few that they are not only the subjects of envy to many, but of suspicion. The world is so mean that, unless it happen to know an unselfish man personally, it hears of his good deeds only to inquire what and how much he expects to make by them. Is not this unpopularity of the human race with itself rather humiliating? Knowing the fact and the reason of it, let us try to inaugurate a better condition of things.

XXVII.

THE LORD'S BUSINESS.

"The children of this world are wiser in their generation than the children of light."

"Business is business."

"Money is wise; it knows its own way."

I SUPPOSE my minister—the Rev. Theodore Dunn—to be one of the very best in New England. If there is any thing that I object to in him, it is his uncomfortable faithfulness. But I have always taken his pointed discourses and his still more pointed personal exhortations in good part, as I know him to be the best friend I have, and an honest and thoroughly enthusiastic worker in his holy calling. A few weeks ago I received a note from him, requesting me to call at his study for private conversation upon an important topic. I was promptly at his door at the time ap pointed, and spent a very pleasant evening with him. The special subject upon his mind was the importance of conducting all business enterprises upon Christian principles. I think he must have heard something of my connection with a fancy scheme which it is not necessary for me to mention here; but he had good breeding, and said nothing about it. I could do nothing, of course, but accede to his excellent propositions, and bow to his exhortations. I may say, before going further, that he was entirely in the right, and that I hope his lesson has done me good.

After returning home, I thought the matter over. This was the seventh time he had sent for me, for the purpose of lecturing me. I had had some thoughts on the subject of religion which I had never expressed to him, and said to myself, "I will turn the tables; I will send for the minister." I gave no time for second thoughts, and dispatched a note on the instant, requesting him to call at my office "for private conversation on the subject of religion," on the following evening. I was in my office at the time appointed, and my minister came in sight as the clock struck seven. He greeted me cordially, but was evidently a little puzzled. He took the seat proffered him, threw open his overcoat, and in certain commonplace inquiries, indicated his wish that I should commence the conversation. I felt a little awkwardly in the position into which I had voluntarily thrown myself; but, determined to make the best of it, I assumed the censor and adviser, and opened.

"Mr. Dunn," said I, "you invited me to your house to talk to me, in your sacred capacity, of the importance of conducting business enterprises on Christian principles. I have invited you here to-night to talk to you on the importance of conducting the Christian enterprise on business principles."

Mr. Dunn smiled good-naturedly, and bade me proceed.

"Well, sir," said I, "I am a business man, and have had, in a somewhat active life, considerable knowledge of great enterprises; but I consider the Christian enterprise as the largest operation ever undertaken by human hands. It contemplates nothing less than the peaceful subjugation of a rebellious world to the forsaken rule of heaven—the restoration of a degenerate race to purity and happiness."

"But it is not man's enterprise," said Mr. Dunn.

"Hear me through, sir. Moral forces, of varied nature and operation, and supernatural influences, as the most of us believe, enter into the prosecution of this enterprise; but beyond these I recognize an element of business—an element inherent in every thing which can legitimately be called an enterprise. An enterprise in any sense is a business enterprise in some sense, because it involves management and machinery. Christianity has its parish, its society, its officers and organizations of various sorts, its missionary associations, and its educational institutions. Is it not so?"

Mr. Dunn simply bowed, and said, "Go on."

"To the management of the business department of the Christian enterprise are called such men as have the most practical business tact—men who add to general intelligence, social position, piety, and zeal, that acquaintance with the men of the world, and that familiarity with the forms, details, and maxims of the world's business, which will enable them prudently and efficiently to perform their duties. This is a thing of men and money, and when money is short, and men are scarce, you will admit that management becomes a thing of great importance."

I saw that my visitor was becoming interested. He laid off his overcoat entirely, and drew his chair nearer to me.

"Now," said I, resuming, "we must settle, at starting, exactly what the Christian enterprise is. Is it building up our church?"

"O no!" replied Mr. Dunn, "certainly not."

"Is it building up our sect?"

"Not by any means."

"Well, suppose you tell me, in a few words, what

it is," I suggested, for the purpose of leaving the burden with him, and getting my premises.

"I should say," replied my minister, "to be concise, that the Christian enterprise is the enterprise of converting the world to Christ."

"A good answer," I responded. "I accept your definition, for it is my own; and I knew you could give no other. Now, I am not going into theology at all. It is enough for me to know that eighteen hundred years ago, a remarkable personage appeared, who was allied alike or in a degree to divinity and humanity, and who declared himself to be the Saviour of the human race. I will not differ with you, or with anybody else, as to how his salvation was to be conferred. I know that he possessed a supernal elevation of character, that he lived a spotless life, that he gave utterance to the noblest precepts and principles, that he was crucified by cruel men, and that he rose again. His great mission, announced beneath the conscious pulses of Judea's stars, was that of the bearer of good-will to all mankind. The commission which he gave to his disciples was, 'Go ye into all the world and preach the Gospel to every creature.' He began the enterprise, and intrusted its completion to the hands of his disciples. This is the enterprise which they have undertaken; the enterprise which you, Mr. Dunn, have defined. As I look at it, it is a grand, overruling, all-subordinating scheme. If its merits are equal to its pretensions, there is not, under the whole heaven, any great work which should not be subordinate to this."

I had grown a little warm with my talk, and my minister smiled in his own pleasant way, and remarked that he thought I had mistaken my profession. I bade him wait until the conclusion before committing himself on that point. I then resumed.

"In examining the operations of the propagators of Christianity, I find that money stands as the basis of nearly all of them. Money builds the church, hires the minister, sends the missionary, prints the Bible, drops the tract, supports the colporteur, and furnishes the life-blood of all the Christian charities. Without money comparatively nothing can be done, and co-ordinately essential are men; for without ministers, and missionaries, and colporteurs, and printers, money, devoted to this enterprise, would be fruitless. The question is, therefore, as to how this money and these men are used? Can you think of an instance, Mr. Dunn, in which money has been misused?"

"I was just thinking," he replied, "of the little town of Montford, up here, which has four church edifices and not a single minister."

"Yes," said I, "and there is Plum Orchard, just beyond Montford, which contains three ambitious-looking church edifices with a poor minister in each—

very poor, I may say, in more than one sense. In Montford, sectarian zeal has actually exhausted all of the available means of Christian effort, and, so far as I can learn, the town has not for years been the scene of the slightest Christian progress. There are four flocks there without a shepherd. Plum Orchard contains twelve hundred inhabitants. Half of these do not attend church at all, partly because they have become disgusted with the sectarian strifes that have prevailed among the churches, but mostly because the preachers (poor men!) have no power over them. Of the remaining half, a moiety attend church in a thriving manufacturing village two miles distant, and three hundred are left to fight out the bootless battle, which keeps three inefficient leaders in commission, and does good to no one. Only the first case is an extreme one. Similar cases are found everywhere. Now, Mr. Dunn, do you blame an unbelieving business world for laughing and scoffing at a spectacle like this?"

"Very bad, very bad!" sighed my minister with a sad face and a shake of the head.

"Now, sir," I resumed, "I am not going to say that this is not right, for I pretend to hold nothing deeper than a business view of it. I am not going to say that it is not just as the Head of the church would have it; but I must say, very decidedly, that, viewed in its business aspect, it is the most foolish, the most inexcusable, the most preposterous profligacy. The whole world cannot illustrate such another instance of the squandering of precious means by organized bands of sane business men. I say this in view of the fact which, in courtesy, I am bound to admit, that it is all done conscientiously, and for the simple purpose of pushing forward, in the most efficient manner, the Christian enterprise."

"We must have charity, sir," said Mr. Dunn, in a wounded tone.

"Charity!" I responded, somewhat warmly, for I saw that he had not fully comprehended my meaning; "what has charity to do with it? I have impugned no man's motives. I am simply criticising a business operation. Let me illustrate. Suppose that I have a business which extends throughout this State. I have an article to dispose of which should be in the hands of every man within its limits. I cannot visit every town and every man myself; therefore I must avail myself of a system of offices and agencies. Proper agents being scarce, it becomes necessary for me to economize. What, therefore, shall be my policy? Evidently so to apportion my offices and agents as to bring the commodity I have to dispose of within the reach of all, if possible—of the largest possible number, at least. I hold my agents strictly responsible to me for the manner in which they do my work. I require of them all to hold up their hands and swear to do it faithfully and well; not striving for precedence or monopoly, not seeking their own aggrandizement, but laboring directly to forward my interests and advance my enterprise. This is a plain business operation; and, stripping the Christian enterprise of every thing foreign to its business element, I place it by the side of that enterprise as a just standard by which to judge it. Jesus Christ has something to dispose of to every individual of the human race. In order to bring it to the knowledge of every individual, he has established a system of offices and agencies, and committed the work of extending them over the world to his people. He requires of every agent that he shall devote himself, with a single purpose, to the forwarding of his great enterprise—the conversion of the world. But his agencies, after the lapse of more than eighteen hundred years, have been established only upon a small portion of the territory, and difficulties seem to clog the path of their further progress. We find his followers, all of whom profess a supreme wish to forward his enterprise, disagreeing upon some of the minor and non-essential details of the business, dividing themselves, and using up the money which he has committed to them in building a multitude of splendid and often rival offices, and retaining in each an agent, while a large portion of the field is entirely unprovided for. Shut up within the walls of a small partisanship, they seem to have lost sight of the great enterprise to which they have committed themselves; or, if they sometimes think of it, it is with a piteous lamentation over the hinderance of a cause in the way of which they have placed every possible business obstruction."

"We must have charity," reiterated Mr. Dunn, moving uneasily in his chair.

"Now, my good sir," I rejoined, "as you are determined to make me a censor of motives, rather than a critic of policy, I will not have the name without the game—you know the old saying. So, when I say that the business part of the Christian enterprise is badly managed, I will say that, if a business of mine were managed thus, I should come to the conclusion that my agents care more for themselves than they do for my business."

"I saw where you were coming," replied Mr. Dunn, with his kind smile, for he was determined to make a sort of enemy of me before he could be complacent.

"Well, sir, you brought me here," I replied "Now let me go on. It is a confessed and patent fact that money is short and men are scarce. The call is uttered and echoed in every quarter of the world for more money and more men; but is it too much to say that enough of both have been squandered in the business management of the Christian enterprise to have carried Christianity into every household? The money expended in church edifices, and inefficient governmental church establishments, and bootless and worse than bootless controversies, and the upbuilding of rival sects, would have crowned every hill upon God's footstool with a church edifice, and placed a Bible in every human hand. Further than this: if the men now commissioned to preach the gospel were properly apportioned to the world's population, millions would enjoy their ministrations who never heard the name of Jesus Christ pronounced, and never will. The towns in Christendom which feebly support, or thoroughly starve, two, three, or four ministers, when one is entirely adequate for them, are almost numberless."

"Yes," said Mr. Dunn, "I believe that statement is true. I suppose I could preach to this whole town in which we live, as well as to my limited congregation."

"Precisely, Mr. Dunn. Now do you suppose the business world around us here can look on and see how we manage, and not see the thriftlessness and inconsistency of the whole thing? And if this business world should happen to conclude that men who profess what we do, and manage as we do, are not in earnest, would it compromise its reason and its common sense by it?"

"But I thought you to be a lover of art, and always glad to see fine church architecture," responded Mr. Dunn, endeavoring to shift the burden.

"You are entirely correct—I wish the world were full of it; but I am talking now as a business man. I understand that a church is built with a supreme desire for the service of Christianity—as something which is to tell directly upon the Christian enterprise. It is a simple question of dollars and cents. Do one hundred thousand dollars, expended upon a church edifice, half of which is devoted simply to ornamental art, exert over fifty thousand dollars in power toward the conversion of the world?—for we must always come back to this definition of the great enterprise. This is what churches are built for, as I understand it; and I ask whether, in this case, fifty thousand dollars are not absolutely lost to the Christian enterprise? Is there not within the bounds of Christendom enough of bricks, and mortar, and mouldy marble, and costly spires, and flaming oriels, and gorgeous drapery, and luxurious upholstery, and chiming bells, and deftly-chiselled stone, all dedicated nominally to the service of Heaven, to enrich the whole world with Christian light, were it economically dispensed?"

"There is undoubtedly something in what you have said," replied my minister, "but I think not so much as you claim. And now, as you are so apt at tearing down, suppose you try your hand at building up."

"I do not see that this is needful, for the remedy is indicated by the disease; but if you wish it, I will do it willingly. As a business man, it will be impossible for me to judge of the relative importance of maintaining a certain truth or tenet, acknowledged to be non-essential, and the saving of a human soul. That is for you to do. I only take the enterprise in gross; and I say to you, as one of the managers of the Christian enterprise, that if you are supremely devoted to that enterprise, if the great and only end you seek be to compass the salvation of the world, then you will spend your money and apportion your means in such a way that the enterprise shall feel their whole power. Here, for instance, in this town, we have four religious societies. These happen to be Episcopal, Congregational, Methodist, and Baptist. All these people expect to meet each other in heaven. They call themselves 'Evangelical Christians,' thus acknowledging that non-essential differences of belief keep them from thorough fraternization. These men are made a common Christian brotherhood by the common reception of what they deem to be the essential truths of Christianity. One large church and one good pastor, like you, Mr. Dunn, would be sufficient for all these sects. Now, as they can agree upon the essential truths of

Christianity, why may they not do so formally, and leave to every man that Christian liberty of opinion upon the non-essentials which belongs to him, and which by right of public charter or private choice he will exercise under all circumstances. From my knowledge of human nature I might go further, and say that such an exhibition of united devotion to a great cause as this would be, and such a demonstration as it would furnish of the real, fraternal spirit of Christianity, would accomplish more for the Christian enterprise than the separate labors of the four sects could hope to accomplish in a quarter of a century."

"My dear sir," said my minister, warmly, and with tears brimming his eyes, "this is a beautiful dream of yours. I say it from my heart, I would gladly see it realized; but there are so many prejudices to overcome—there are such different modes of thought and worship—I do not see how we could come harmoniously together."

"Ah! but, Mr. Dunn, I have only spoken on the supposition that all prejudices had been subordinated—all partisan feelings and non-essential opinions—to the Christian enterprise. I have only suggested such a management of the Lord's business as I should insist upon if it were mine; and I repeat what I have said, in effect, before, that if, in the enterprise, which I had supposed my own, I should find three or four offices in opposition to each other, in any form, carried on by as many agents, each claiming the preference, with no essential reason for difference, I should conclude that they cared more for themselves and their opinions than they did for my business. In the method of reform which I have suggested, I would liberate and render available a vast amount of idle capital, and I should find upon my hands a large corps of agents to be sent into such portions of the field as might be un supplied. I would also divert the large annual outlay which it has cost to support these superfluous institutions into the maintenance of the new efforts incident to their transplantation."

"This looks rational, however impracticable it may be," responded Mr. Dunn, half doubtfully. "But is this your whole plan?"

"Hardly the shell of it, Mr. Dunn. Are you weary?"

"Bless you, no!" replied my minister, pressing my hand. "I was only going to remark, that there would still be men wanting."

"Very well," I replied. "I thank you for leading me to this point. Every year the religious press breathes out the stereotyped lamentation that only a few young men, comparatively with the wants of the world, are graduated at the theological seminaries. While young men by tens of thousands throng every avenue of trade.

and press into every alley that leads to an avenue, and while the professions of law and medicine are crowded with the ambitious and the talented, few adopt the noblest calling of all, and the Christian enterprise lags for lack of public laborers. Now I have yet to see the first branch of business in this country, or in any country, that cannot command as many men as it will pay for. I tell you that for money I can obtain men for any service under heaven—any service that I would engage in—good, Christian men, too. Money will send men into the eternal ice of the poles, under the fires of the equator, across snow-crowned mountains, and among savage beasts and savage men. What, by the way, is the amount of your salary, Mr. Dunn?"

"Eight hundred dollars a year."

"That is more than any other minister in this town enjoys, and it is just half the sum I pay my head-clerk. Now, be kind enough to tell me what is expected of a minister."

I had touched the right chord, and my minister rose to his feet, and gave it to me, "with an unction."

"It is required of a minister," said he, "that he shall possess a first-class mind; that he shall spend ten of the best years of his life in that crucifixion of the flesh which efficient study necessitates; that, if poor, he shall carry into his field of labor a load of debt which will gall his shoulders for years; that he shall withhold himself from all other callings and all side schemes and sources of profit; that he shall write from two to three sermons each week, and preach them; that between Sabbath and Sabbath he shall attend two or three evening meetings; that he shall visit every family in his parish once in six months; that he shall take the laboring oar in all public charities; that he shall call upon the sick, and look after strangers, and officiate at funerals, and serve as a member of the school committee, and deliver one or two lectures before the village lyceum every season, and visit the sewing-circle, through the winter—and—"

"And all," I continued, rising also to my feet, for a sense of injustice was getting the better of me, "and all for a sum at which a modern railroad conductor would snap his fingers in contempt."

But Mr. Dunn was at home in this matter, and I was very glad to let him talk for me.

"I will not amend your conclusion of my sentence," said my minister, smiling, "though it is not exactly in my style. I will say, however, that a minister's salary is usually adjusted to the lowest current cost of living. In this way, he is allowed to lay up nothing for paying off his debts, furnishing his house, stocking and replenishing his library, educating his children, and surrounding himself with the convenient and graceful externals of cultivated life. The pastor, enfeebled as he is by care and the preparatory studies through which he has passed, is required to be the hardest drudge in his parish. He is accepted as a laborer in the most important calling that honors our poor humanity, he is loaded with responsibilities which call for more than human strength for their support, yet his scanty stipend is doled out to him more as if he were a dirty beggar, than a messenger from heaven, and the almoner of its choicest gifts."

Thus having honestly poured out his heart and his convictions, my minister sat down. I resumed my seat also, and, as I did so, I said, "Mr. Dunn, is it to be wondered at that so few men can be found who are willing to enter upon a life like this?"

"But, my dear sir, there are higher considerations," said he, hastily recalling himself. "I declare it to be the highest evidence I have known of the benignly constraining power of Christianity, that so many men can be found who are willing to leave the brilliant paths—open to all—of honor, wealth, and fame—to leave them with the dew of youth upon their brows, and their hearts bounding with the strong pulses of young manhood, and take this dusty road, parched with penury, thick strewn with the thorns of ingratitude, and thronged with humiliations, from the valley where it diverges from the world's great track, to the heaven-touched hill where the weary feet strike upon the grateful, golden pavement."

"You are right, entirely right," I responded; "and now I wish to say to you that I consider the Church, in its business capacity, an unjust and grinding master towards those whom it has called into its service. Its noble colporteurs are not paid as well as hod-carriers, and you have told me feelingly how well its pastors are paid. And I say that, in a business point of view, the lamentation over the small supply of pastors in preparation is childish and contemptible, so long as the commonest business principles are disregarded in the endeavor to secure a larger supply. You speak of higher considerations. I grant that there are such considerations, for I have evidence of them in the fact that there are any ministers at all. But what have a church and religious society to do with those considerations in hiring a minister? If they find their candidate an educated, sound, spirited, honest, and devoted man, they accept him, and enter into a business relation with him. They are a laboring, producing, trading congregation, with all the avenues of wealth opened to them. They have no right to ask him to give them one cent. In the salary they give him, it is their duty to yield him a full share in their prosperity. Any thing less than this makes him a menial, and does him injustice. Now it may be that ministers do not care about money, but I have noticed that our few well-paid pulpits never go begging for ministers. They are all undoubtedly exercised by other considerations, but as the Christian enterprise is a common one, the Church has no more right to require them to devote to it their life for higher considerations than money, than they have to demand money for higher considerations than their services. It is an even thing."

"I recognize the intrinsic justice of your position," responded my minister, after a pause, "but I am afraid money enough could not be found to conduct the Christian enterprise in this manner."

"But money enough is found to manage it badly," I replied, "and I believe there is money enough to manage it well. I have yet to find the first worldly enterprise that promised safety for investments that did not command all the money necessary for its consummation. Wherever the angels of promise and progress lead, money follows and does their bidding. It builds magnificent cities, and bridges rivers, and excavates canals, and constructs railroads, and levels mountains, and equips navies, and furnishes countless hosts with the enginery of war. In its ready and prolific power, it often furnishes facilities for business before business demands them. The Christian world is flooded with wealth. There is money enough and to spare, and I very decidedly declare, that if, in the subordinate enterprises of Christian life, there is no lack of money, there can be none in the Christian enterprise itself, provided, of course, that Christians are sincere in their expressions of supreme devotion to that enterprise."

"A new test of piety," interpolated my minister.

"Perhaps so, but I cannot help it; because, as a business man, I know perfectly well that any enterprise in which large bodies of men feel a great and absorbing interest, can command all the money which it requires. And now, when the business world sees the Christian world begging for money with which to forward its great enterprise, and counting its receipts by slowly accumulating thousands, what must be the impression of that business world in regard to the honesty and earnestness of that Christian world? Can it resist the quick conclusions of its acutely educated judgment? When it sees a body of men lauding a scheme or enterprise in which they will make no deeper investment than they feel obliged to make for decency's sake, it calls it contemptuously 'a bogus scheme.'"

"You have a grain of truth in a bundle of sophistry, here," replied Mr. Dunn. "It is true, and it is not true. The comparison which you institute between investments in human enterprises and the Christian enterprise is an illegitimate one."

"I see where the trouble is," I rejoined. "The result of the comparison is the wholesale conviction of the Church of the sin of hypocrisy; but I will relieve that of its point by the charitable admission that these men are laboring under a hallucination. I believe they have entire consciousness of sincerity. Still, from my point of view, I can only decide as I have decided. As a business man, I know that the Christian world can command any amount of money it may be desirable to command for the prosecution of the Christian enterprise; and I can only conclude that, if it fail to do it, it is because it has little confidence or little interest in it."

"But do you comprehend the severity of this judgment?" inquired Mr. Dunn, solemnly.

"I do, sir, but I am not responsible for it. I cannot help it. You come to business men for money. Why should we help you to a penny, when you will not invest in your schemes yourselves? You remember how it was when our bank was chartered. We opened the subscription-books, and the stock was all taken in two hours. We believed in our own scheme; but you profess to regard religion as something better than money; you even admit that pastors should labor for higher considerations than money; and yet, when a subscription-book is opened for the advancement of some special interest of the Christian enterprise, Christians almost universally play shy of it, and oblige it to go painfully and pitifully begging for months."

As I concluded, my minister heaved a deep sigh. I feared he was becoming tired of the interview, and expressed the fear to him. He begged me to go on, however, and declared that his interest in my conversation had deepened from the first, although he felt sick and sad with the reflections awakened in the latter part of the discussion.

"We will leave the home field, then," I resumed, "and change the current. I find that, independent of carrying on the Christian enterprise within Christendom, there is a missionary work—a work of aggression upon the domains of heathenism. In this work the business department assumes an importance which it holds in no other section of the scheme of Christian propagandism. The organizations are larger and more powerful, heavier amounts of money are entrusted to them, and a more complicated system of machinery is called into operation. Their operations are two-fold, comprising acquisition and diffusion, and rendering necessary a double set of machinery—one to collect funds, and another to disburse and consume them. These organizations cannot be sustained without a considerable outlay of money, and the amount of money contributed for direct use in forwarding the Christian enterprise must be reduced by the amount necessary for carrying on the machinery of these organizations. This, in itself, is right, as every branch of business should be made to pay for itself. I find, on examining this missionary field, that it is occupied by a large number of organizations, all professedly laboring for the same object."

"A blessed object it is, and may they all be prospered in it!" interrupted my minister.

"Amen! say I; and I will say more than this. From the nature of the case, the grand end of Christian effort is kept more prominently in view in missionary operations than in any other. Selfishness and partizanship are more thoroughly subordinated. The work is one of measurably pure Christian benevolence. Not so much anxiety is felt for the propagation of sectarian views as in the home department of Christian labor. Accordingly, in some instances, we have a union of various organizations for the purpose of saving the expense of operating multiplied sets of machinery."

"You like this, I suppose," said Mr. Dunn.

"Entirely; and simply because it is the business way of doing things. You remember that a short time ago a traveller, in passing over the New York Central Railroad, from Albany to Buffalo, was obliged to purchase a long string of tickets, which represented six or seven—more or less—railroad corporations. Each had its board of officers, its independent set of machinery, its separate engines, cars and men. The business of these lines was to help the passenger on from Albany to Buffalo. Their interest was identical. So business men became aware that there was a great waste in the management. They therefore agreed to a grand scheme of consolidation, by which the whole track should come into the ownership of one corporation, and be placed under one board of management. This was the work of business men. Now these missionary corporations are the managers of roads that lead from earth to heaven; and, unlike the old railroad corporations, they keep up (to speak it reverently) entire routes of transit from one extreme to the other. In this thing, all Christians feel that it is of more importance that a heathen should come to a practical knowledge of the Christian life, than that that life should be accompanied by any special sectarian views. What I wish to say, as a business man, is, that not a cent of money should be wasted in superfluous organizations and machinery, and that all these men who are carrying on this superfluous machinery should be put directly into the aggressive field of operations, where men are so much wanted."

"I agree with you in the main, my friend," said Mr. Dunn, drawing a long breath.

"Yet I only advise in the home field the policy which you approve in the foreign.'

"I know," replied my minister, "but you do not comprehend all the difficulties."

"Who made the difficulties?"

"Let us not go back to that," said Mr. Dunn, smiling.

"Very well, I will go on. We have, scattered here and there, over the land, petty societies, established for the accomplishment of some minor, special ends. There are some of these which must use nearly or quite all the funds they receive in sustaining themselves. Their agents occupy our pulpits, they haunt our houses; and as we do not know them, or the organizations which they represent, we regard it as a hardship to bestow our charities upon them. Speaking in a business way, a hat is a hat, and a human soul is a human soul, wherever found. If I have money to give for the benefit of a human soul, I choose to give it where it will tell directly upon that soul, and not to a man who will keep half of the sum to pay himself for getting it out of me. In other words, I would support that man as a missionary, and thus give the heathen the benefit of his time and my money, rather than deprive the heathen entirely of the one and half of the other."

"Then you would kill all these societies, would you?"

"I would do this: I would place the best business men at the head of our leading charities, and then, if they should fail to find these minor fields of sufficient promise to warrant an outlay in their behalf, I should advise that they remain uncultivated"

"But I do not see," said my minister, "how you will avoid the necessity of keeping up a full corps of collectors. Every church must be approached with explanations and solicitations."

"Yes, but not necessarily by professional collectors. If Christians really feel the interest which they profess to feel in missionary operations, they will need no explanations—no annual posting up in missionary matters. A business man needs no such annual posting up in financial affairs. He reads the foreign news, the price-current, the daily condition of the money-market, and every thing which directly or indirectly bears upon his business. The Christian world has its "Missionary Herald," and other publications, in which all the facts are stated weekly, monthly, or quarterly. Any man really interested in this enterprise, as every Christian professes to be, would of course read these publications with anxious avidity. The pastor does, at least; and I should greatly prefer, Mr. Dunn, to hear a missionary sermon from you, than the tedious harangue of a stranger. At any rate, if the church is really interested in the missionary work, it will gladly assume the task of collecting its own funds, and thus turn into the direct channel of Christian effort the money now expended in supporting collectors, and, with it, the collectors themselves."

Here Mr. Dunn took out his watch.

"Mr. Dunn, I accept the hint. I have bored you."

"Not at all, sir," replied the good-natured man. "I assure you that the act was involuntary. Go on."

"I think," said I, resuming, "that there are but two points more which I care about touching to-night. We business men think a great deal of business honor. In the business world, a man who refuses to pay his just debts is accounted no better than a swindler. All confidence is withdrawn from him, and all business accommodations are refused to him wherever he is known. It was only last Sabbath that you gave out a hymn which had in it this noble stanza:—

'Were the whole realm of nature mine,
That were an offering far too small;
Love so amazing, so divine,
Demands my soul, my life, my all.'

I noticed several eyes around me grow moist with its effect. I have no doubt that the whole church looked upon it as an eloquent expression of their indebtedness to their great Master. They mentally credited Heaven with an infinite benefit, and debited themselves with their entire spiritual, vital, and worldly estate. Now I, as a business man, see that the Christian acknowledges the receipt of this benefit, and in his covenant, or contract, agrees to make the utmost payment in his power. Mr. Dunn, you know I mean no irreverence when I say that the church has not treated Jesus Christ with any thing like the business punctilio which it exercises towards and exacts of its neighbors, and that, if Jesus Christ were the manager of a bank, every obligation the members have given would have passed to protest long ago. I do not pretend to canvass moral obligations, and I will only add, that when the Christian enterprise shall receive all the men and all the money pledged to it by contract, when Christians shall discharge their plain business obligations, voluntarily assumed, and long over-due, there will be no lack of agents or of means for carrying the Christian enterprise to the grand consummation which awaits it."

"This is a new view," said my minister, with enthusiasm, "and should be urged from the pulpit. It must be effective."

"You are welcome to it," I replied.

"And is my lesson concluded?"

"Not quite. I wish to add that business men, in their steady look-out for the main chance, are always on the alert for any incidental or side schemes of profit or advantage that may present themselves. In the Christian enterprise, or among its results, there is such a thing recognized as Christian brotherhood. It ought to be the best and purest relation which can exist between man and man, and, if fully realized, certain material benefits would be sure to result from it."

"What, for instance?"

"Well, you know that, for the purpose of securing benefits that would naturally flow from a genuine Christian brotherhood, various special organizations have been established, such as the Free Masons and the Odd Fellows. Suppose I were in New Orleans, or London, and should fall sick. Suppose, also, that I were a member of your church, and also a Mason. Should I call upon a member of the church first, in order to secure care and aid?"

My minister blushed, and did not reply.

"You know I should not. Now I say that there is a very large class of minds which judge of the soundness of a principle by the character of the action it inspires. To such a class as this, which organization—the church or the lodge—would seem to possess within it the most powerful principle of practical fraternity?"

"But, my dear sir," said Mr. Dunn, warmly, "these societies have nothing good in them that they did not take from Christianity."

"That is it exactly. They have stolen your capital. As a business man, I say that Christianity cannot afford to render necessary or desirable a set of organizations which tend to throw it into disrepute, by doing the work which it is the duty of the church to do.

Were I to undertake a large business, and attempt to manage it in all its details, and so far fail in one of them that another should spring up, and take it out of my hands, and execute it better than I had ever executed it, I should not only feel personally humiliated, but I should feel that my whole business had been wounded. I say, then, that the prosecutors of the Christian enterprise cannot afford to be surpassed by any other organization in the practical results which flow from the brotherhood it establishes. And now, if you will allow me to finish at a breath, I will add that this same business view of brotherhoods applies with equal force to all the organizations formed to do the work which the church neglects to do. Various societies of reform that have sprung up in the past have found their birth in the quick sensibilities of men who have had no connection with the church, and who, in carrying them forward, have met with so much immobility in, or absolute opposition from, the church, that they have become impatient and disgusted, so far, in some instances, as to become open enemies of the church, and even of the Bible itself. I say that the Christian enterprise cannot afford this. Every good principle or purpose which is involved in these side-schemes is taken from Christianity; but Christianity, while furnishing capital for these schemes, loses not only the capital, but the credit of using it, and often has the misfortune to see its thankless beneficiaries turning against it. I say such management as this is ruinous."

"Management, management, management!" exclaimed Mr. Dunn, rising to his feet, and taking his hat from the table—"nothing but management."

"My good sir, what do you mean?"

"I mean this, that your constant association of management with the Christian enterprise is repugnant to my ideas of the nature of that enterprise. The Christian enterprise is heaven-born. It has inherent, irresistible strength, and God is with it! It *must* win its way, if its facts and its principles be proclaimed; and because that in it are the wisdom and the power of God, it does not need the aid of such small management as we apply to our business affairs—still less the aid of that power which the cunning tactician employs in other and less worthy fields of operation."

"I honor the sensitiveness and sensibility in which your words originate," I replied; "but I join issue with you. There is nothing more dangerous to any enterprise than an overweening confidence in its strength. Now, my good sir, against a good cause, interest, lust, and malice manage, and when they crush it, as they have crushed many good causes, they crush it by management. They cannot oppose it on its own merits, and they therefore avoid its issues. But all the power which a good cause possesses within itself resides in its issues. If its opponents be not brought to meet these, it is powerless. Here is where management becomes necessary to meet management, and the nature of the cause and the nature of the opposition will determine the nature of the management."

"But this has nothing to do with business—we were talking of business management."

"I am coming to that. The strictly business management stands upon a different basis. No matter how good or how strong a cause may be, the scheme of its propagation necessarily has its business department, which, being independent of the cause itself, in the fact that it is incident to all organized human action, must be conducted on business principles. I therefore say that there is nothing more dangerous to a cause than that degree of confidence in its strength which makes it responsible for more power than resides in its issues, and leads to the abandonment of departments of labor essential to its success—departments only legitimately to be operated by human sagacity and human prudence."

As I closed my last sentence, the clock struck nine. I felt ashamed for having detained my good friend so long, and apologized, not only for this but for the almost disrespectful act of calling him to me. He said that no apology was needed, that I had given him food for thought for many days, and that I must not be surprised to see a portion of my thoughts reproduced in the pulpit, with such modifications as reflection might suggest. I helped him on with his over-coat, and he left the door in a brown study.

About three weeks afterwards he called upon me, and desired me to remain at home on the approaching Sabbath morning, as he should use so many of my thoughts in his discourse that it would embarrass him to have me present. I acceded to the request, on the condition that he would give me his sermon to peruse after its delivery. This he agreed to, and the arrangement was fulfilled in all its parts.

The sacred text upon which he founded his discourse was this: "For the children of this world are wiser in their generation than the children of light." It was an eloquent performance. All my views had been modified somewhat, by passing through the medium of a more spiritual mind: but they had not been shorn of their power. The closing paragraphs impressed me as powerful and eloquent, and I trust that their author will take no offence at my purloining them and publishing them here.

"I see the Christian enterprise only feebly aggressive, pushing on laboriously here and there, and counting its gains slowly, while the great worldly enterprises among which it floats dash proudly before the wind with sails all set, until they ride, staunch and trim, in the harbors for which their owners destined them. Think you that in a world of business like this any enterprise can succeed that is not managed in a business manner? Why should the children of this world be wiser in their generation than the children of light? Why will the latter vainly call upon God to work miracles in their behalf, while refusing to apply to the Christian enterprise those simple, common-sense rules of policy and action, without which (they well know) their own business would fall into irretrievable ruin? What sight more pitiable can there be, than a band of mistaken Christians, praying Heaven for help in favor of a cause the laws of whose progress they utterly ignore or positively transgress?

"Incidentally our discussion has touched something deeper than this. Heaven has chosen the weak things of this world to confound the things which are mighty; and the business test which we have applied to the Christian enterprise, and its managers and management, low and subordinate as it is, has reached down into the great Christian heart, and tried its sincerity. It has shown plainly, if it has shown any thing, that the real nature of the claims of Christianity is but feebly realized by its professors. It has shown that Christians are repudiators of their acknowledged debts, and that behind all this business delinquency and dishonor there must be a torpor of moral sensibility and a lack of moral honesty, sufficient, but for the upholding arm of a pitying Heaven, to crush the Christian enterprise into the dust.

"As I look out upon the field of Christian labor I see nothing harder to accomplish than what has been accomplished already. There is not a difficulty there which, in the progress of the enterprise, has not been many times surmounted. The entire practicability of the Christian enterprise has been demonstrated by the work already done. The Christianization of mind is not a more difficult process now, than it has been in the past. If, therefore, the great difficulties in the path of the Christian enterprise do not exist in the field through which it passes, where do they exist, where can they exist, save among those who are carrying it on?

"I feel oppressed and humiliated by the secondary position which the great enterprise to which I have devoted myself is allowed to occupy among the teeming enterprises of the world. I am ashamed that there is no more practical sagacity manifested in its management, and that even the readiness and freeness of the grace of God are called in question to account for a barren adversity of results, for which the Christian world is alone responsible.

"Every interest of man calls for the efficient prosecution of this enterprise and its speediest completion.

The moral and intellectual health and the redemption of a race are involved in it. Whatever of blessing there may be in wealth, whatever of honor and purity there may be in politics, whatever of sweetness ther may be in family and social relations, whatever of worth there may be in manhood and womanhood, whatever of dignity and true joy there may be in worldly pursuits, whatever of glory there may be in the wide range of human action, depends upon results which this enterprise shall achieve for mankind. It should be broad, instinct with action, heaven-reflecting, and world-embracing like the sea. Upon its billowy bosom the navies of all lands should ride. The keel of every human enterprise should be sunk deep in its waters, and every sail should be filled fully and steadily by the benign breezes that sweep over its surface. It should only break against great continents of Christian life or islands of human happiness, kissing their feet in the tidal throb of its heaven-born impulse, tempering the fervors of Prosperity's summer, meliorating the rigors of Adversity's winter, and binding the nations in peaceful communion through the medium of its flexible and universal element. The world cannot live without this enterprise. Wherever upon its surface a true civilization has lifted its head above the dead level of barbarism, there you may trace the footsteps of the Christian enterprise. Wherever the divine man has conquered the brute, there has stood the messenger of heavenly truth.

"What is true in the past will prove true in the future. Thus, then, the world's destiny and the world's hope are in the Christian enterprise. And how is that enterprise managed? What progress is it making? In this view, how pitiful and contemptible, nay, how sinful and damnable, become the strifes of words, the wars of sects, the dumb formalities, the droning imbecilities, the treasure-sacrificing ostentations, and the niggardly meannesses of the great mass of those who have in charge this heavenly enterprise! May the day soon dawn, when the great object of Christian labor—the conversion of the world—shall reconcile all differences, unite all hearts and hands, and lead on victoriously to the consummation of a scheme which had its birth in the bosom of God's great benevolence, and shall find its issue in universal joy!"

XXVIII.

THE GREAT MYSTERY.

"Consider well and oft why thou camest into the world, and how soon thou must go out of it."

"Careless men let their end steal upon them unawares and unprovided."

"Our birth made us mortal; our death will make us immortal."

"He that fears not the future may enjoy the present."

WHY was I—why were you—called forth from nothingness into a world of danger and pain, and sin and death? That is a question that has blistered the lips of a million wretches, and we who are happier, though still the subjects of evil, may well ask it, and consider it.

The earth has been the subject of two grand experiments, and in the results of these we are to find the answer, if anywhere. Six thousand years ago two persons—a man and a woman—were born into the world, and awoke to the consciousness of existence. They were pure and good, and so pure and so good that they were open to free intercourse with God and with spir itual intelligences. Their tent was the blue sky, the floor of their dwelling was carpeted with Eden's grass and flowers, and fruits, heaven-provided, hung on every hand. They knew no danger, they felt no pain, they were free from guilt, and had no fear of death. They were adapted to drink in happiness from the things around them, and the things around them were adapted to supply their desires. A pair of perfect bodies, a pair of pure spirits, they found themselves in what seemed to be, and was to them, a perfect world. They were made in the image of God, and were therefore free. This freedom was essential to their perfection, their dignity, and that development to which their Maker looked as the crowning excellence and glory of those whom He would call his children.

But there could be no such thing as right without its opposite—wrong; and no good without its opposite —evil. They were free, and could obey the laws placed upon them, and thus perpetuate their happy estate, or they could do wrong, and blast it. They yielded to the first temptation to do wrong, and found themselves and the world transformed. This first experiment contemplated the development of humanity into its highest form and noblest quality without the ministry of evil. It was a failure, and God, who instituted the experiment that we might answer the great question we are considering, knew it would be. It was brief, terrible, and decisive. The parents and representatives of the race were driven out of the garden, and they and all their posterity have been subjected to a new experiment—a better and a safer one. It was better that Adam and Eve should fail then and there, than a thousand years afterward. The experiment was tried under the most favorable circumstances, and did not succeed. That was enough for the world. There had been experiments before—how many we know not—but we know that there were great beings who had failed to keep their first estate, and had done immeasurable mischief in the spiritual universe. The Bible tells of these.

The new experiment—that of which all of us are the subjects—contemplates the introduction of the race into its highest estate through the vestibule of evil. We are to take evil at this end, and not at the other. We are to become familiar with sin and its effects, to overpower temptation, to become "perfect through suffering." We are to win strength by struggle, and to have our love of that which is good developed side by side with our hatred of that which is bad. Our spiritual natures are to be knit into firmness by toil, to be hardened into power by conflict, to be softened into humility by the experience of their weakness, to be rendered tractable by affliction, and thus fitted for a safe eternity. What do you say of this experiment? Is it not a grand one? Is it not a benevolent one? Tell me not of the millions who fail of this! I leave them in the hands of that benevolence that has devised such great things for you and for me. That this is the exact motive of the experiment now in progress in this world, I have no doubt; and I do not believe, considering the length of time it has been persevered in, and the nature of the agencies that have been introduced, that it will prove to be a failure. If I did, I should lose all faith in God. I believe that the world, as it is—considering the nature and duration of our existence and the nature of ourselves and the service and society for which we are designed—is the best and safest world we could be placed in. There I leave it.

Well, is this existence, which I have entered upon by no act of my own, on the whole a blessing? Do you feel it to be so to you, or not? How would you like to be annihilated—to be wiped out as a conscious existence, and plunged into the dark nothingness from whence you came? You shrink from the thought, and so do I. Why? Because, and only because, we believe, with all healthy souls, that existence is a blessing. We love life, here and now, in this world of sickness, sorrow, and death. If, then, existence be a blessing, little or large, to us, and we were born into a world of suffering and of sin for the purpose of fitting us to live safely and securely through all the coming ages of our existence, certainly it becomes us to take it contentedly, to front our destiny boldly and trustfully, and see what we can make of it. We are to consider not only why we came into existence in such a world as this, but how soon we must go out of it, and how brief, at longest, the period of this momentous experiment will be.

If this world be not a place for education of some sort, it has little meaning. The idea that a man should be placed in the circumstances that surround us, and subjected to this great experiment without reference to another existence—that he should die as soon as he has learned to live—is simply absurd. Admitting, then, that we are the subjects of education, how does it become us to see that the end of its period do not steal upon us unawares and unprovided. How does it become us, as rational men and women, to make the most of our life, and to see that in our case, at least, the experiment be successful. The man who receives life as a blessing, to be cherished and loved, and enjoyed and preserved, is a coward if he be afraid to consider its intention and its end, and a guilty spendthrift if he let it pass by, month after month and year after year, without securing the education it was meant to convey.

This wise providence of time and opportunity becomes the more desirable when it is remembered that it is only when we are fearless of the future that we may enjoy the present. The lamb doomed to slaughter on the morrow, gambols and rejoices in freedom to-day, because it is fearless of the future. The bird sings, the insect hums with the joy that is in it, the kitten frisks upon the carpet, not because they are not subjects of pain and death, but because, knowing nothing of them, they have no fear of them. A fearlessness of the future identical with this cannot be ours, and the fact is proof of our higher destiny; but a fearlessness of the future, which will render our life far happier than theirs, may be acquired, by preparation to meet the future. Life is only an inestimable blessing to him who, prepared to meet the future, and who, comprehending his position and the meaning of it, is not afraid of the future.

The shadowy future—ah! how many shudder when they think of it! How many shrink from even the thought of it! How it poisons every present delight, and embitters every pleasure, and haunts every hour of hollow mirth! I declare this to be utterly unnecessary—even inexcusable. We are content to live here in this world of sorrow and pain, and shrink from a world in which it shall be done away with, if we are only manly enough to get ready for it! Accepting our life as an experiment—a period of education—entering into the plan by which we are to be fitted for everlasting happiness and safety, and subjecting ourselves to the necessary discipline—we lift the great shadow from us; the phantom of the future retires, and, calm in our trust, we live in the present a life of enjoyment. No man can enjoy life in its full, blessed measure, until this tormenting fear be cast out; and it can never be cast out by a rational man until the future looks safe to him. The moment the future is taken care of, present trials seem small, and present joys are lifted to our lips, their divine aroma unalloyed.

The tendency of religious instruction and of philosophical speculation has been to mystify us all upon this problem of evil in the world. Our preachers have talked solemnly upon the subject of "reconciling" the existence of evil with the infinite love and goodness of God, as if the belief in this goodness and the recognition of this evil in the ordained system of things, were to be regarded separately, with an unbridged gulf of darkness between them. Threading that darkness, fathoms below sight, there is supposed to be a chain of golden links, holding one to the other, to be apprehended only by an irrational faith. Such teaching and such speculation are full of miserable infidelity. I, for one, believe in the infinite love and goodness of God. I plant myself on them, and I believe that I could not be shaken from my foothold without the wish that I might plunge into annihilation. On this firm rock I take my stand, and, without seeking to reconcile the evil which enters into my experience and comes within my observation with God's love and goodness, I seek rationally to account for the evil as an appointed means of the infinite love and goodness. I know God is good, or He is no God; and I believe, as a natural consequence, that I am to be raised into assimilation with the specific quality of His goodness by rational knowledge of, and experimental acquaintance with, evil. I call that infidelity, and not faith, which makes of the existence of evil a blind mystery, to be mournfully accepted, and sacredly kept from the hand and eye of reason. It makes no difference what events and what destinies hinge upon the existence of evil here; it matters nothing what sufferings, what woes, what sorrows assail us; the moment we swing loose, by the smallest remove, from perfect trust in the infinite love and goodness, and a belief in the benign ministry of evil as a department of their means, we lose our hold upon the meaning of our life.

Believing in God's goodness and His infinite and everlasting love, I believe in evil, as a part of the divinely appointed means by which my soul is to be educated and disciplined for its highest possible destiny—as a means rendered necessary by my nature and by my destiny. I believe that if now, in my soul's infancy, I make my acquaintance with evil, and grow up through it into my soul's manhood—learning its relations to divine law and to my own personal, godlike freedom—that I shall be safe through the infinite ages that stretch before me. I shall not be like the angels who lost their first estate, and plunged, full-fledged, from heights of heavenly power into an infamous perdition. God might as well have given me my infancy in heaven as here, if evil had no ministry of good for me. I might as well have been ushered at once into the spiritual life, as to have been the tenant of a death-doomed body, if there had been nothing to be gained by probationary subjection to the power of evil.

So I take my life as I find it, as a life full of grand advantages that are linked indissolubly to my noblest happiness and my everlasting safety. I believe that infinite love ordained it, and that, if I bow willingly, tractably, and gladly to its discipline, my Father will take care of it. I say nothing here of the Christian scheme, because I choose to discuss this single question by itself.

Now, what I wish to say, is this: that a man who decides that God is infinitely good, that he was born into a world of evil because it was, on the whole best for him to be born into such a world, that evil has a ministry for him essential in the nature of things to his highest destiny and his completest safety, and, with faith and confidence, accepts his lot and makes the most of it, has nothing to fear in the future, and nothing to hinder his enjoyment of the present. From such a man the incubus of a dark future is lifted. The future may be undefined and, perhaps, in some sense, awful, but it will not be terrible; for infinite love will take care of it. The terror inspired by things to come thus taken out of the way, the ban on present happiness is removed, and soul and sense may drink in unreproved, whatever good that crowds to them for acceptance.

If we, finite creatures, encumbered with flesh, and harassed by its appetites and gross proclivities, conquer the temptations that assail us, and find ourselves growing stronger and better as we grow older; if, in this world of evil, and in a measure through its ministry, we become elevated and ennobled, how safe and glorious must that future be which shall find us free from the appetites that chafe us, and released from all pain and sorrow! Now, is it not worth something to make that future so secure that we can approach it with fearlessness? Ah yes! The life which is, no less than the life which is to come, is ours, if we will take it. With this lion in our way removed, how sweetly will taste the pleasures of life! How precious will become the loves that our hearts drink so greedily, and often so fearfully, when we know that we may drink them forever! How charming will become the songs of birds, and how fragrant the perfume of flowers, to him who believes that he will only lose them to listen to angelic music, and breathe the breath of flowers that never decay!

Much of the mystery that hangs over the world, as a world of evil, grows out of a misconception of the highest life. If the highest good of the short years that are allotted to us on the earth be happiness, then is the existence of evil indeed a mystery; but it is not, and cannot be. Happiness is a legitimate object of life, and I am even now endeavoring to show how more of it may be secured; but it is an object to be held subordinate to the education necessary for service in another realm, and the permanent enjoyment of another estate. I believe that the truest happiness of the world is to be found in heartily accepting and entering into the scheme by which evil is made a powerful agency in the development and eternal security of the soul. Accepting this ministry, and trusting in the goodness—profound and eternal—in which it was conceived, what a flood of light and love is let in upon the soul! No! there is something better for us in this world than happiness, whatever there may be beyond. We will take happiness as the incident of this, gladly and gratefully. We will add a thousand-fold to the happiness of the present in the fearlessness of the future which it brings, but we will not place happiness first, and thus cloud our heads with doubt and fill our hearts with discontent. In the blackest soils grow the richest flowers, and the loftiest and strongest trees spring heavenward among the rocks.

THE END.

www.ingramcontent.com/pod-product-compliance
Lightning Source LLC
LaVergne TN
LVHW010146110826
845151LV00002B/442
9781425537395